COFFEE LOVE

50 WAYS TO DRINK YOUR JAVA

DANIEL YOUNG

WILEY

John Wiley & Sons, Inc.

To the memory
of my father,
David Young.

Copyright © 2009 by Daniel Young.

Photographs copyright © 2009 by Daniel Young. All rights
reserved.

Book design and composition by Ralph Fowler / rlf design

Published by John Wiley & Sons, Inc., Hoboken, New Jersey

Published simultaneously in Canada

For general information on our other products and services or for
technical support, please contact our Customer Care Department
within the United States at (800) 762-2974, outside the United
States at (317) 572-3993 or fax (317) 572-4002.

Wiley also publishes its books in a variety of electronic formats.
Some content that appears in print may not be available in
electronic books. For more information about Wiley products,
visit our web site at www.wiley.com.

Library of Congress Cataloging-in-Publication Data:
   Young, Daniel.
      Coffee love : 50 ways to drink your java / Daniel Young.
         p.   cm.
      Includes index.
      ISBN 978-0-470-28937-2 (cloth : alk. paper)
         1. Coffee drinks. 2. Coffee. I. Title.
      TX817.C6Y68   2009
      641.3'373—dc22
      2008016832

Printed in China

10 9 8 7 6 5 4 3 2 1

ACKNOWLEDGMENTS

The greatest reward in undertaking this project came not only from interviewing people passionate about their craft but also in the pleasure of having a coffee with them. I am indebted to all those who proved to me (as I hope this book will do for you) that there is a correlation between the quality of the coffee and that of the conversation. Special thank yous to David Schomer of Espresso Vivace, Marino Petraco and Moreno Faina of illycaffè, Susie Spindler of Cup of Excellence, Manuel Terzi of Caffè Terzi, Anita Le Roy of Monmouth Coffee Company, Johanna Wechselberger of Mocca Club, and Rob Fischer of the Palo Alto Creamery. I also relied on the know-how of world barista champions Tim Wendelboe and Fritz Storm, cocktail king Dale DeGroff, the outstanding food reporter and Roman guide Iris Carulli, the culinary historian Richard J. S. Gutman, the chef-restaurateur Zarela Martinez, and All Hungary Media Group editor/publisher Erik D'Amato.

Credit and warm thanks are owed to the cafés who granted me permission to photograph on their premises: Caffè al Bicerin, Trieste, cover photo, pages iii and 77; Flat White, London, pages i and 23; Café Sperl, Vienna, pages ii and 78; Café Diglas, Vienna, page vi; Colonial Café, Milan, page 1; Mocca Club, Vienna, pages 3, 11, and 27; Espresso Vivace, Seattle, page 7; Victrola Coffee, Seattle, page 10; Caffè Terzi, Bologna, page 13; Climpson & Sons, London, page 15; Fernandez & Wells, London, page 16; Gimme Coffee, New York, pages 21 and 25; Caffè Sant' Eustachio, Rome, pages 32 and 35; Addie's Thai Café, London, page 41; Monmouth Coffee, London, pages 43 and 85; Kavárna Obecní dům, Prague, pages 61 and 105; Caffè Florian, Venice, pages 63 and 64; Café Central, Vienna, page 69; Gresham Kávéház, Budapest, page 74; Central Kávéház, Budapest, page 78; Eagle Bar Diner, London, page 79; Spilia Beach Café, Hydra (Greece), page 89; Nizza, New York, page 95; Daphne's, London, page 101; Sevilla, New York, page 103; Café Slavia, Prague, page 113; Match Bar, London; page 115.

I benefitted enormously from the professionalism of the culinary team at Wiley led by my insightful editor Linda Ingroia. I am thankful to Ava Wilder for guiding this book through the production process, to Ralph Fowler for his imaginative design, to copyeditor Lisa Story for her careful work on the manuscript, and to Charleen Barila and Cecily McAndrews for helping resolve the day-to-day dilemmas. My deepest gratitude to my agent, Alice Martell, for her acumen and dedication.

I enjoyed the love and support of my mother, Mimi Young; my brothers, Bill Young and Roy Young; my sisters-in-law, Sharon Baumgold, Laurie Young, and Gill Constantinopoulos; my nieces, Liz, Hava, Molly, and Shoshana; and my nephew, Aaron. And I cannot imagine a more perceptive sounding board or more loving co-conspirator than my wife, Vivian Constantinopoulos.

CONTENTS

INTRODUCTION

Nothing both unites and divides us like coffee—the world's favorite beverage, after water. The aroma of coffee is as universal a signal of daybreak as the rooster's crow and a far better reason to get out of bed. The popular pick-me-up is a fixture at work and an instrument of leisure. Great with company and great company when you have none, coffee makes the world a far less lonely place.

But coffee also stimulates division. There are a dozen or so basic brewing methods to distinguish cultures, myriad preparations and variations to delineate subcultures, and millions of personal preferences and idiosyncrasies to identify each typically atypical coffee consumer. Drinkers who flip their lid because their 8 A.M. cup is a few sugar grains short are asserting their individuality while validating this greater truth: No one is in a terribly

good mood *before* they've had their morning coffee fix.

Coffee Love does not exhibit national or regional loyalties, picking sides between two outstanding coffees—Ethiopian Yirgacheffe versus Colombian Bucaramanga—or two classic stovetop coffeepots—the Turkish *ibrik* versus the Italian *moka*. Rather, *Coffee Love* extols the multiplicity of beans, origins, roasts, blends, grinds, brews, and formulas that comprise the coffee universe. It applauds the differences among and within coffee drinkers. It embraces habit and whim, tradition and trend. It appreciates that coffee preferences are personal, situational, and experiential, and can be as much about the where, when, and with whom as about the brew itself. Then again, sometimes it *is* all about the bean.

Coffee Love does confess to a fixation on the cream of the coffee crop, in the most literal sense. Foamy cream and creamy foam toppings are the alternately rich, velvety, silky, smooth, and sensuous hallmarks of so many wonderful coffee styles, from the reddish brown *crema* of an espresso to the dark brown *kaimak* of a Turkish coffee, to the mahogany-colored froth of a French press coffee, the pristine white *schlagobers* (beaten cream) of a Viennese *Einspänner*, or the tan-highlighted white microfoam of a cappuccino. When it comes to coffee, very small bubbles are a very big thing.

This book takes a wide view of the bean universe via close-ups of coffee subjects, know-how, ideas, places, and conversations, and how they are all reflected in the enticing liquid surface of a cup. At its heart is a recipe for more division; fifty recipes, in fact—fifty great ways to have your java.

But, please, you decide how much sugar to add.

Coffee's Family Tree
From Abyssinia to the Bean Belt

The origins of the coffee plant may be traced to the highlands of Ethiopia, formerly known as Abyssinia. A popular legend attributes its discovery to a goatherd named Kaldi whose weary flock became so peppy after nibbling on the berries of an exotic tree that they began dancing on their hind legs. Unable to resist temptation, Kaldi sampled the mysterious plant and felt the same stimulation. He shared his discovery with a monk, who, fearing the berries were the work of the devil, flung them into the fire. An irresistible aroma wafted through the monastery and into the night air.

As early as 600 A.D., coffee spread from its botanical home in Ethiopia to the southern tip of the Arabian peninsula, now known as Yemen. Originally the red berries, each the size of a small cherry, were chewed. Around the thirteenth century A.D., the Arabs began to roast, grind,

and brew the green coffee beans found inside the berries. The taste for this beverage followed pilgrims and traders north from the Yemeni port of Mocha, the trade hub whose name would come to signify coffee, to Mecca, Medina, and Damascus.

Dutch traders smuggled a coffee plant out of the Yemeni port of Aden and replanted seedlings first in Ceylon and later in the colony of Java, now part of Indonesia. Over time, the Dutch and other colonial powers explored further opportunities for coffee as a cash crop: the Dutch in Dutch Guiana; the French in Martinique, French Guiana, and the Antilles; the Spanish in Puerto Rico and Cuba; and the British in Jamaica and India. Coffee was introduced into Brazil illicitly through a romantic liaison between a Brazilian lieutenant colonel, Francisco de Melo Palheta, and the wife of French Guiana's governor. Palheta bid farewell to his lover and returned to Brazil with a bouquet in which she had hidden coffee seeds and cuttings.

More than fifty countries within the so-called bean belt between the Tropic of Cancer and the Tropic of Capricorn possess the climatic and geological conditions necessary for coffee production. Two species of coffee are cultivated for commercial use: *arabica,* which comes in many varieties, and *canephora,* commonly known as *robusta,* its predominant variety. Arabica grows best at high altitudes in subtropical temperatures. Constituting more than 70 percent of world production, arabica's major producers are Brazil, Colombia, Indonesia, India, Mexico, Guatemala, Uganda, Ethiopia, Peru, and Costa Rica. Robusta thrives at lower altitudes in Vietnam, Brazil, Indonesia, India, Guatemala, Uganda, and the Ivory Coast, amassing higher yields and lower prices than arabica.

Roasting and Profiling
Light, Medium, Dark, or Some of Each

The main characteristics of coffee flavor—aroma, acidity, body, and taste—are dramatically affected by the process of roasting. In a standard drum roaster, the green coffee beans are fed by a hopper into an oven whose rotating motion insures even roasting. As their internal temperature rises, the beans dry to a pale yellow and then gradually expand and change color to progressively darker shades of brown, much like a slice of bread heating in a toaster. Italians, in fact, use the verb *tostare* (to toast) to describe

the roasting process. Coffee beans crack for the first time when their internal temperature reaches about 380°F (195°C). At this point, the beans have doubled in size and assumed a light brown color. The second crack occurs at about 440°F (225°C), when the beans have acquired the color of a medium-dark roast.

So, what is happening to the flavor of the beans as they cook? A *light roast* has bright acidity, light body, minimal aroma, and little or no bitterness. With a *medium roast,* the acidity is more balanced; the body, fuller; the aroma, more pronounced. As the coffee approaches a *dark roast,* the acidity diminishes, and the bitterness emerges and eventually dominates. Roasting decisions can be a trade-off. In Finland, where per capita coffee consumption is the highest in the world, the near-universal preference for a light roast reflects a taste or tolerance for a pronounced acidity and a distaste or intolerance for any bitterness. The Neapolitans, who opt for the fullness and bittersweet flavor of a dark roast in their espresso, sacrifice the zesty acidity. Allowing for personal and regional tastes, the artisanal roaster develops a roasting profile for each bean "varietal" (genetic subspecies), setting roasting temperatures and times best suited to the varietal's specific traits. The heat source itself can be a factor. At Mr. Espresso, a family-run roasting company in Oakland, California, the 240-kilo and 460-kilo roasters are fired with white oak. Roastmaster John Di Ruocco insists that slow-roasting with oak eliminates some unpleasant flavors and can produce a darkish espresso roast that is not too bitter. When asked if the fired oak imparted a smoky taste to the coffee beans, as it does to pizzas baked in a brick oven, Di Ruocco shook his head. *That,* apparently, was too much to ask for.

Coffee Revolution in Seattle
Creating Art, Making Waves

The development of the specialty coffee trade can be divided into three waves: pre-Starbucks, Starbucks, and post-Starbucks. The first coffee wave was driven by loyalties to mass-marketed brands sold at supermarkets and unbranded brews poured at truck stops. The second wave began in ripples at local coffee shops that promoted their superior freshly roasted coffees by assimilating the culture of the Italian espresso bar to enhance the coffees' preparation and enjoyment. Indeed, it was the experience more than the coffee that was gradually diluted when one such second-wave pioneer, Starbucks, expanded from a single store—opened in Seattle's Pike Place Market in 1971—to a 15,000-outlet empire. The depersonalization of Starbucks was reflected in its decision to install automatic, push-button espresso machines requiring little knowledge from the baristas operating them. Starbucks chairman Howard Schultz was critical of these changes in "The Commoditization of the Starbucks Experience," a widely leaked memo he sent to the company's board of directors in February 2007. "We overlooked the fact," he noted, "that we would remove much of the romance and theater that was in play."

The primary movers of the third wave have been microroasters who source their beans from small farms, roast them in small batches, and expect their baristas to educate customers about the

characteristics and origins of their coffees and coffee blends. Approaching their selections as wine merchants would their prized bottles, the microroasters speak of *terroir*, referring to the microclimates and other geographical factors that affect the qualities of a bean varietal. Their counterpart to wine tasting is cupping, a process for evaluating several coffee samples side by side. In the back room of Victrola Coffee Roasters in Seattle's Capitol Hill district, roaster Jodi Geren spoons coarse coffee grinds into up to twenty glasses (two per sample) and tops them with near-boiling water. The saturated grounds float to the surface to form a crust. With nose lowered to glass, she breaks the crust with a tasting spoon to release and inhale the trapped aromas. Next, she fills the spoon with the liquid beneath the crust and slurps it to aspirate the coffee over her tongue and reveal its flavor profile.

It is left to the front-line baristas to connect the customer to the chosen bean. Within the meticulous, click-clacking flurry of the brewing task, there is one discreet action that demonstrates the loving touch of expert baristas: They actually feel the coffee, running their fingers over the grinds to smooth out air pockets and dense clumps before brewing a shot of espresso. A more open display of their passion is evinced in the hearts, rosettes, and other patterns they craft on the surface of lattes and cappuccinos.

This imagery exploits the tendency of the frothy steamed milk and *crema*-topped espresso to flow in waves. While pouring the milk into the espresso, the barista lightly and rhythmically shakes the pitcher to manipulate those waves and create the desired shape. David Schomer, Seattle's great exponent of what's called latte art, views the baristas who work beside him at Espresso Vivace not as geeks but rather as artists who exhibit tolerance for the human condition. A thick skin is more of a job requirement than the tattoos that habitually cover it, especially in the morning. "You're dealing with people who are pre-coffee," Schomer notes.

Beyond his ephemeral art form, Schomer had been preoccupied for two decades by a single pursuit: an espresso that tastes as good as freshly ground beans smell. After analyzing espresso-brewing techniques and equipment, he at last found a locally made commercial espresso machine with which he could accomplish that elusive goal.

Mark Barnett was making processing equipment for gutting salmon before he began equipping a hotter industry with a foothold in the Pacific Northwest. In 1995 he initiated domestic production of La Marzocco, the Ferrari of commercial Italian espresso machines, in Ballard, Washington, turning out up to seventy-five units per month for Starbucks alone. But the plant shut down not long after Starbucks dropped the La Marzocco machines in favor of push-button models in 2003. Barnett then decided to design and build his own machines, giving prominence to their hand-operated levers, rather than their digital temperature controls, to emphasize their manual

operation. With polished stainless steel body, clean lines, and no ornamentation, the Synesso Cyncra was ergonomically designed to function as an extension of the person using it. Schomer "pulled" some of the Cyncra's first espresso shots (the terminology derives from the manual levers on piston espresso machines that have to be pulled down to build the necessary pressure) and described the sensation of their *crema* as "a pat of butter melting on your tongue."

Though Barnett must have felt a quiet satisfaction when he read how much Starbucks's Schultz regretted replacing the machines Barnett had once built for him, he holds no grudge. "We have Starbucks to thank for this industry," says Barnett.

Coffee and Caffeine
The Half-Life to a Better Life

The ever-growing list of potential benefits researchers have associated with coffee consumption includes the obvious and the not-so-obvious: pleasant stimulation; a mind-racing jump-start; mood elevation; greater alertness and memory; the prevention of drowsiness; the alleviation of headaches; enhanced performance in athletic competition; increased effectiveness of pain-relieving medicines; protection against lung, skin, and colon cancer; a reduced risk of type 2 diabetes and Par-

kinson's disease; the prevention of dental cavities; and the alleviation of asthma symptoms. Although the antioxidants and other compounds naturally present in coffee beans play a role, studies show that a large share of these benefits can be linked to the caffeine in coffee. Caffeine, the most widely consumed pharmacologically active substance in the world, must also take the hit for some of coffee's less desirable effects, including insomnia, irritability, hand trembling, and rapid heartbeat.

The amount of caffeine in a cup of coffee varies according to the preparation method, the volume and strength of the serving, and the characteristics of the beans used in the grind. Some noteworthy distinctions:

- Beans of the robusta variety are about 50 percent richer in caffeine than arabicas.

- Coffees brewed in a French press, a Turkish *ibrik*, or a percolator have less caffeine than drip coffees that pass through a paper or metal filter.

- A single espresso shot has lower caffeine levels than a single serving of basic drip coffee.

Coffee delivers caffeine to the blood in a hurry. It takes only about fifteen minutes to take effect and another fifteen to thirty minutes to reach the period of peak concentration in the plasma. The amount

of time it takes for the effects to wear off varies, however, particularly after the first few hours. Consequently, researchers refer to the "half-life" of caffeine—the time required for the body to eliminate one-half of consumed caffeine. They estimate a half-life at three to four hours for nonsmoking adult males, and up to 50 percent less time for smokers. The caffeine half-life is much higher in women taking oral contraceptives and in pregnant women.

Coffee Bean Basics

The Choices

A coffee bean is the seed of a berry from trees of two species, *coffea arabica* and *coffea canephora*, which produces the "robusta" variety. The flavor, aroma, complexity, and balance of the finest highland arabicas are judged vastly superior to the often harsh, rubbery notes of most robustas. Roasters may, however, add some robusta to their espresso blends to increase an espresso's body and volume of *crema.*

Most of the world's finest arabicas are cultivated in one of three coffee-producing regions: East Africa, Asia Pacific, and Latin America. The beans of Ethiopia, Kenya, and Rwanda are prized for aromas redolent of berries or citrus, whereas those from Central and South American plantations stand out for their clean, sweet flavor and crisp acidity. Arabicas from the islands of Indonesia yield full-bodied coffee with smooth acidity and earthy flavors. Beyond these generalities, the taste and character of beans are affected by climate and soil, which vary from country to country, farm to farm, and harvest to harvest. In specialty coffee shops, single-origin and single-estate coffees, indicating unblended beans from a single region, cooperative, or farm, are often identified by their place of origin, as in Costa Rican Tarrazú (a region in the Central Valley of Costa

Rica) or Colombian Mesa de Los Santos (after an organic farm in Colombia's Santander region). Coffee beans, like wine grapes, may also be classified by varietal, a genetic subspecies with its own set of characteristics. *Arabica* varietals such as Typica and Bourbon show significant regional differences, hence the importance attached to the geographic labeling of coffee beans.

Storage

Roasted coffee should be protected from moisture, air, heat, and light in airtight, opaque canisters. Ground coffee loses its freshness much faster than roasted whole beans, which, when stored at room temperature, will stay fresh for a week, or possibly two. The best storage solution is to buy up to a week's worth of whole beans and store them at room temperature. If you need to keep beans for two weeks up to two months, store them in the freezer, never the refrigerator. Transfer them to a freezer bag, squeeze out the air, seal, and then wrap the bag in plastic wrap. Do not remove the beans from the freezer until you are ready to grind them.

Grinding

Because ground beans get stale quickly once exposed to air, the best thing you can do for your coffee is to grind the beans yourself immediately before brewing. A secondary benefit of a home grinder is the heady aroma emitted as roasted beans are ground. (Coffee grinder aromas truly must rank with sizzling bacon and baking chocolate chip cookies among the world's most enticing food scents.)

There are basically two types of electric coffee grinders, blade and burr. Only the burr models will produce a preset, uniform grind (essential for espresso). The beans are crushed between two burrs, one stationary, the other spinning from the motor. In blade grinders, a spinning blade pulverizes the beans. There are no grind settings. The longer you let the blade spin, the finer the grind will be. Blade grinders do an adequate job, but the extra $100 or $150 spent on a burr grinder by Gaggia, Baratza, Mazzer, or Rancilio may be the wisest investment you can make in a coffee appliance.

Tasting

A simple way to develop your nose and palate is to sample two coffees side by side. For a clearer comparison, choose single-origin beans rather than blends and keep secondary factors constant. If you were to compare a light roast coffee with a dark roast, you could end up evaluating the characteristics of the roasts instead of the beans. Experts recommend preparing the tasting samples in a manual cone filter brewer or a French press to facilitate an assessment of these four traits:

- aroma (earthy, chocolaty, nutty, herbal, etc.)
- body (the way it feels in the mouth)
- flavor (the overall perception)
- acidity

Not to be confused with sourness or bitterness, a crisp acidity can enliven a coffee, much as it can a white wine, bringing a zesty effervescence to the cup. Its tang, felt as dryness under the edges of the tongue and at the back of the palate, might also be associated with the pleasing tartness of berries, citrus, and green apples.

Choosing a Coffeemaker

The first thing you want your coffeemaker to do is maintain water at the proper brewing temperature. It sounds like so little to ask, and yet so many machines disappoint. If the water is not hot enough you will fail to extract all the flavor from the coffee. Boiled water will overextract the grinds, releasing bitter oils into the brew. You are in fact more likely to brew a correctly extracted coffee with a manual, single-cup cone filter holder or a non-electric drip brewer by Chemex, Bodum, or Melitta than with some automatic coffeemakers costing up to five times the price. The water temperature and flow in electric drip machines can be irregular, while their warming plates can scald the coffee. Still, if heating water in a kettle to a precise temperature is not what you care to be doing first thing in the morning, the automatic drip coffeemakers by Technivorm-Moccamaster will hit the right spot: They are certified by the Specialty Coffee Association of America (SCAA) to brew at the proper temperature.

One worthwhile alternative to both manual and automatic drip coffeemakers is the French press pot (page 46). Another is the increasingly popular vacuum brewer. Resembling some kind of glass apparatus in a mad scientist's lab, these so-called vac pots consist of a lower chamber for the water, an upper chamber for the coffee grinds, and a filter-lined siphon tube to connect them. As the vac pot heats over a stove or spirit lamp, the water climbs first in temperature and then in its chamber, rising up through the siphon to make initial contact with the grinds. Steam pressure eventually pushes the water up into the upper chamber to steep the grinds. When the heat is removed, the pressure drops, and the brewed coffee is sucked back down into the lower chamber, leaving the spent grounds behind in the filter. Manual stovetop vac pots by Yama and Bodum cost as little as $35 to $70. Cona vac pots, each with its own alcohol-burning spirit lamp, sell for $200 to $260.

Moka stovepot espresso pots (page 30) make strong coffee and cost as little as $15. But for true espresso with a rich layer of *crema*, there is no low-cost alternative to a pump-driven home espresso machine with a bar pressure of at least 15. Super-automatic machines, starting at about $500, grind, dose, and tamp the coffee with the push of a button. Semi-automatics leave these tasks to the home barista. Gaggia, Saeco, and la Pavoni make reliable models in the $300 to $500 range, but it's the Rancilio Silvia, at about $600, that makes reviewers rhapsodize, and the La Marzocco GS3, at $7,500, that makes even professional baristas drool.

Some machines accept pods or, in the case of the Nespresso system, capsules filled with precise amounts of ground coffee. These offer convenience at the expense of control: You cannot regulate the grind, dose, or tamping pressure; and your selection is restricted to only those blended and single-origin coffees prepackaged as pods.

Water

You can master bean basics and still spoil your coffee by using bad water. A cup of black coffee is 98 percent water. If you don't have good tap water, run it through a water filter to remove the unpleasant tastes and odors. Or use bottled water, preferably purified water or spring water with a low mineral content.

THE ESPRESSO BAR

Espresso

For the Love of Coffee and Crema

THE FIRST TASTE OF ESPRESSO is like "enveloping the tongue in velvet pajamas," according to David Schomer of Seattle's Espresso Vivace, or having "our tongues painted with many little droplets of oil," in the words of Marino Petraco, a senior research scientist at illycaffè and a lecturer at the Università del Caffè in Trieste, Italy. That's how two coffee authorities from two coffee capitals describe the silky coating left on the taste buds by the first deposit of espresso *crema*. *Espresso*, Italian for "express," can be explained as "fast coffee." The word is also associated with *espressamenta*, meaning "expressly" (as in a coffee "expressly for you"). Whatever the interpretation, espresso indicates the high-pressure extraction of coffee. And the thick surface layer of reddish-brown *crema* is the hallmark of a well-prepared cup.

No espresso machine can extract desirable aromas—caramel, chocolate, floral, fruity, smoky, earthy—not already present in the coffee. Not the first espresso machine, a steam-driven cylindrical prototype patented in 1901 by Italian engineer Luigi Bezzera. Not the piston-driven

mechanism first manufactured in the late 1940s by Achille Gaggia, nor the pump-driven models developed since. But the *macchina* is one of the four *m*'s—the others being the *macinadosatore* (grinder-doser), *miscela* (blend), and *mano dell'operatore* (barista)—essential to getting the best from the beans. A carefully chosen blend of complementary coffees is customary for espresso. While single-origin espressos can be revelations, the balance, richness, and harmonic complexity of a quartet or quintet is generally preferred to the narrower range of a soloist. Blend or not, the rate of extraction—the time it takes for the water to flow through the packed coffee grinds—is critical: Too fast, and you won't get all the flavor. Too slow, and you start picking up unpleasant tastes. Petraco estimates the ideal extraction time as 20 to 30 seconds. Schomer says 23. The barista can adjust the flow either by changing the grind or by altering how tightly he or she tamps the coffee particles in the portafilter.

A desire to master the art of preparing espresso brings baristas from all over the world to the Università del Caffè in Trieste. Its main lecture hall is an audiovisual theater with tasting tables, video conferencing, and up to four interpreters sitting behind glass booths, translating Petraco's Italian poetry into various languages. The name of the school is misleading: To complete a degree takes not four years but four days. However, a four-day education is just about right when *espresso* is your speed.

The Espresso Warm-up

As the high-pressure sprint of coffee brewing, espresso needs a good warm-up. These preliminary steps, included in the following master recipe, quickly become second nature. When preparing espresso for cappuccino, latte, or other espresso-based coffee drinks, remember to:

- Warm up not just the machine but every part that comes in contact with the espresso: filter basket, portafilter, cup (or glass).

- Before tamping the coffee grinds in the portafilter, feel them with your fingers, dispersing or flattening out any clumps to ensure a smooth flow.

ESPRESSO

MAKES 1 SERVING • A single shot of espresso should measure between 1 and 1½ ounces (between 30 and 45 ml). To prepare a double shot or two single shots at once, double the dose of coffee grinds and use a larger double-serving filter basket intended for that quantity. The extraction time for single and double shots alike is 20 to 30 seconds, the espresso flowing down from the portafilter like warm honey from a spoon. You can correct the extraction time by adjusting the grind: coarser to speed the flow, finer to slow it. Consider using a light-medium, medium, or medium-dark roast instead of the very dark roast long associated with espresso. The near-blackening of the beans can kill their delicate aromas and cover their nuanced tastes with a bitter char.

> 1 rounded tablespoon (about 7 grams) finely ground coffee, preferably an espresso blend

Turn on the espresso machine, insert the filter basket in the portafilter, secure the portafilter in the brew head of the machine, and leave to warm up for 5 minutes or according to the manufacturer's directions.

Place an empty espresso cup or demitasse under the brew head, turn on the brewing switch, and fill the cup with water to preheat the cup. Turn the brewing switch off and empty the cup, then remove the portafilter and wipe the filter basket dry.

Put the coffee in the filter basket. Feel and level the coffee grinds with your fingers, dispersing or flattening out any tiny clumps. Carefully flatten and compress the coffee with a tamper, first pressing down and then finishing with a twist. Brush any loose grinds off the rim of the portafilter.

Secure the portafilter in the brew head and place the cup under it. Turn on the brewing switch and brew for 22 to 28 seconds, or until the cup is about ½ to ⅔ full with 1 to 1½ ounces of espresso. Serve hot.

MAKES 1 SERVING • Also called *caffè americano* and *café americano*, this is the answer for those of any nationality who want to prepare an elongated espresso that resembles a full cup of drip coffee in volume and strength. To triple or quadruple the amount of water your espresso machine passes through a fixed dose of coffee grinds you would need to prolong the extraction time, thereby admitting unpleasant, bitter flavors. The great Americano way to dilute an espresso is to partially fill a standard coffee cup with near-boiling water and then brew or pour an espresso over it. This process should not be reversed, as pouring hot water over the espresso diminishes the *crema*. The quantities given below may need to be doubled to fill a large mug.

> ½ cup water
>
> 1 rounded tablespoon (about 7 grams) finely ground coffee, preferably an espresso blend

Warm up the espresso machine. Meanwhile, heat the water to a near boil.

Put the coffee in the filter basket of the portafilter, tamp down with a tamper, and secure the portafilter in the brew head. Pour the hot water into a coffee cup. Place this cup, or a brew pitcher or other receptacle, directly under the brew head.

Turn on the brew switch and brew for 22 to 28 seconds to yield 1 to 1½ ounces of espresso. (If using a brew pitcher or other receptacle, pour the espresso over the hot water in the cup.) Serve hot.

Steaming Milk
There Is Foam, and There Is Microfoam

YOU CAN FROTH MILK FOR coffee drinks by heating it in a saucepan over medium heat and beating it with a whisk until hot but not boiling. Or, for about $20, you can buy a battery-operated handheld frother that can double the volume of preheated milk (or cold milk heated afterwards in a microwave) and produce a fluffy head of foam to spoon atop your cappuccino. Plunger-style frothers ($20–$30) also do a satisfactory job of frothing cold milk before it is heated in the microwave. One step up from these are automatic electric frothers ($50–$100). But to generate the high pressure needed to produce "microfoam"—a creamy, velvety-smooth froth composed of only the tiniest, most imperceptible microbubbles—you need a powerful lever-operated or pump-driven espresso machine.

Be sure to consult your espresso machine's operating instructions before proceeding to the guidelines here. Use a stainless steel frothing pitcher, which absorbs heat instantly and lets you gauge the milk's rising temperature simply by holding it with your bare hand. A pitcher whose shape tapers inward toward the top holds the milk better.

1. Press the steam button and wait for the ready indicator light to turn on (or, in some models, off).

2. Turn on (or, in some models, open) the steam valve for a second or two to release any moisture inside the wand, then switch off (or close).

3. Fill the pitcher up to one-third full with cold milk (preferably whole or 2 percent), submerge the tip of the steam wand at least half an inch below the milk surface, and turn the steam back on. Slowly lower the pitcher, thus lifting the tip of the steam wand toward the surface. You want to hold the tip close to the surface but not quite on top of it, and never above it.

4. As the foam rises and the milk's volume expands, gradually lower the pitcher so the tip of the wand remains just below the milk surface, in contact with the milk. Place your free hand on the side of the pitcher

to feel for the heat. As the pitcher begins to heat up, tilt it slightly to create a whirlpool effect inside the pitcher. Continue steaming until the side of the pitcher becomes too hot to hold. If using a thermometer, the desired temperature is 150°F (about 65°C). Turn off the steam while still holding the tip of the wand under the milk surface.

5. Knock the bottom of pitcher on the counter a couple of times and, if necessary, swirl the pitcher to elimi-nate any larger bubbles that may have formed.

6. Very gently pour the steamed milk from the pitcher into the cup in an even, steady flow. Serve hot.

CAPPUCCINO

MAKES 1 ESPRESSO SHOT • This recipe is for an authentic Italian cappuccino. For a larger one, double the quantities. For a milkier cappuccino, increase the milk to 6 tablespoons.

> **1 rounded tablespoon (about 7 grams) finely ground coffee, preferably an espresso blend**
>
> **¼ cup cold milk (whole, 2%, or nonfat)**
>
> **1 pinch cocoa powder or ground cinnamon, optional**

Warm up the espresso machine. Put the coffee in the filter basket of the portafilter, tamp down with a tamper, and secure the portafilter in the brew head. Place a 5- or 6-ounce cup directly under the brew head, turn on the brew switch, and brew for 22 to 28 seconds to yield 1 to 1½ ounces of espresso.

Press the steam switch and wait for the ready indicator to light up. Meanwhile, pour the milk into a stainless steel pitcher. Submerge the tip of the steam wand at least half an inch below the milk surface and turn on the steam switch. As the foam rises, gradually lower the pitcher so the tip of the wand remains just below the milk surface. As the milk begins to heat up, tilt the pitcher slightly to swirl the milk and continue to steam until the side of the pitcher becomes too hot to hold. Turn off the steam while still holding the tip of the wand under the milk surface.

Pour the frothed milk into the cappucino in one of two ways:

- For a smooth cappucino in which textured milk is evenly integrated throughout the beverage, gently pour the frothed milk over the espresso in a thin, steady stream.

- For a cappucino with a foamy head, hold back the foam with a spoon and gently pour the milk over the espresso. Spoon foam over the top.

Sprinkle with cocoa powder or cinnamon, if desired. Serve hot.

Cappuccino and Latte
Telling Them Apart

AN ITALIAN DICTIONARY explains the difference between *cappuccino* and *latte*. Literally, *Cappuccino*, from *cappuccio*, refers to the small hood worn by Capuchin friars. *Latte* is the Italian word for milk. An espresso mixed with milk came to be known as a *cappuccino* owing to the light brown color of the Capuchin friar's habit, or, more recently, as a *latte*, foreign shorthand for *caffè latte* and *caffèllatte*, which both mean "coffee with milk."

From there, the distinctions vary by country, region, and personal taste. It is generally accepted that a cappuccino should have less milk and a thicker, firmer layer of foam than a latte. An Italian cappuccino can be divided into thirds, with equal amounts of espresso, hot milk, and milk foam. Italians regard this as a perfect balance between coffee and milk flavors. In Italy a *caffèllatte* may have no foam at all.

The widely accepted specific formulas in Italy call for a single 30- to 40-ml (about 1- to 1⅓-ounce) espresso shot in both drinks, with 100 ml (about 3⅓ ounces) of frothed milk for cappuccino and 150 ml (about 5 ounces) of steamed milk for *caffèllatte*. The foamier cappuccino requires a 140-ml (almost 5-ounce) cup; the *caffèllatte*, a 200-ml (6¾-ounce) glass or cup.

North Americans and northern Europeans typically prefer bigger espresso shots (or more of them), more milk, and larger cup sizes. It's hard to say if Starbucks's decision to inflate the standard "small/medium/large" sizing with its "tall/grande/venti" selection anticipated this preference or, conversely, helped bring it about. Regardless, you should expect a milkier cappuccino the farther you are from Italy. In the United States, the espresso-to-milk ratio can be closer to 1:4, rising to 1:6 for a latte. Finally, a cappuccino is much likelier to take a dusting of cocoa or, outside of Italy, ground cinnamon, whereas a latte is more often flavored with a sweet syrup.

LATTE

MAKES 1 SERVING

> 1 rounded tablespoon (about 7 grams) finely ground coffee, preferably an espresso blend
>
> ½ cup milk (whole, 2%, or nonfat)

Warm up the espresso machine. Put the coffee in the filter basket of the portafilter, tamp down with a tamper, and secure the portafilter in the brew head. Place a coffee cup, brew pitcher, or other small receptacle directly under the brew head. Turn on the brew switch, and brew for 22 to 28 seconds to yield 1 to 1½ ounces of espresso.

Press the steam switch and wait for the ready indicator to light up. Meanwhile, pour the milk into a stainless steel pitcher. Submerge the tip of the steam wand at least half an inch below the milk surface and turn on the steam switch. As the foam rises, gradually lower the pitcher so the tip of the wand remains just below the milk surface. As the milk begins to heat up, tilt the pitcher slightly to swirl the milk and continue to steam until the side of the pitcher becomes too hot to hold. Turn off the steam while still holding the tip of the wand under the milk surface.

If the espresso is in a brew pitcher or receptacle, pour it slowly into a coffee cup or a 6- to 8-ounce glass. Gently pour the steamed milk over the espresso in a thin, steady stream. Serve hot.

LATTE MACCHIATO

MAKES 1 SERVING • Distinct from both a latte (page 25) and a *caffè macchiato* (page 28), a *latte macchiato* (pronounced ma-kee-YAH-toh, literally "marked milk") is a glass of steamed milk with a middle band of espresso. The espresso settles under the airy milk froth yet over the liquid milk surface, creating a beautiful, three-layered, white-brown-white coffee with a foamy head rising over the glass. It's a nifty effect to create and even more pleasurable to dissolve.

Simple syrup or flavored syrups—caramel, vanilla, almond, hazelnut, berry, chocolate, maple, amaretto—may be added to sweeten a latte macchiato in one of two ways:

- To preserve the layered effect, pour the syrup over the finished drink, and leave it to the drinker to stir and blend it into the milk and coffee.
- To better integrate the syrup into the drink, pour it into the milk before it is steamed.

The quantity of syrup, generally between 2 and 3 tablespoons for a 10-ounce latte macchiato, is dictated by its relative sweetness as well as by personal taste.

> ⅔ cup whole milk
>
> 2 rounded tablespoons (about 15 grams) finely ground coffee, preferably an espresso blend
>
> Simple Syrup (page 85; or substitute flavored syrup) to taste, optional

Warm up the espresso machine. Press the steam switch and wait for the ready indicator to light up. Meanwhile, pour the milk into a stainless steel pitcher. Submerge the tip of the steam wand at least half an inch below the milk surface and turn on the steam switch. As the foam rises, gradually lower the pitcher so the tip of the wand remains just below the milk surface. As the milk begins to heat up, tilt the pitcher slightly to swirl the milk and continue to steam until the side of the pitcher becomes too hot to hold. Turn off the steam while still holding the tip of the wand under the milk surface.

Spoon the frothed milk into a tall 10-ounce glass, starting with the foam on top and gradually working your way down until the glass is full. Let stand, allowing the milk to settle under the foam while you prepare the espresso.

Put the coffee in the double-sized filter basket of the portafilter, tamp down with a tamper, and secure the portafilter in the brew head. Place a brew pitcher or other receptacle under the brew head, turn on the brew switch, and brew for 22 to 28 seconds to yield 2 to 3 ounces of espresso.

Slowly pour the espresso into the glass over the center of the foam in a thin stream. Top with syrup, if desired. Serve hot.

CAFFÈ MACCHIATO

MAKES 1 SERVING • A *caffè macchiato* is identical to an *espresso macchiato*, but should not be confused with a *latte macchiato*. A *latte macchiato* is steamed milk "marked" with espresso, as its Italian name suggests, whereas a *caffè macchiato* is an espresso "marked" with a spoonful of milk foam. The stirring of the *caffè macchiato,* creating a moussey mixture of milk and *crema*, and the subsequent licking of the spoon constitute one of the great morning rituals in the Italian espresso bar experience.

> **1 rounded tablespoon (about 7 grams) finely ground coffee, preferably an espresso blend**
>
> **1 to 2 tablespoons cold milk (whole, 2%, or nonfat)**

Warm up the espresso machine. Put the coffee in the filter basket of the portafilter, tamp down with a tamper, and secure the portafilter in the brew head. Place an espresso cup directly under the brew head, turn on the brew switch, and brew for 22 to 28 seconds to yield 1 to 1½ ounces of espresso.

Press the steam switch and wait for the ready indicator to light up. Meanwhile, pour the milk into a small stainless steel pitcher. Angling the pitcher, submerge the tip of the steam wand just below the milk surface and turn on the steam switch. As the foam rises, gradually lower the pitcher so the tip of the wand remains just below the milk surface and continue to steam until the side of the pitcher becomes too hot to hold. Turn off the steam while still holding the tip of the wand under the milk surface.

Spoon the milk foam over the espresso. Serve hot.

THE RANKINGS ARE UNCANNY: Five of the world's six leading countries in per capita coffee consumption are Nordic. Finland, the world leader at 11.4 kilos (25 pounds) per person annually, is followed in the International Coffee Organization (ICO) rankings by Iceland, Norway, Denmark, and Sweden. The unrivaled Nordic thirst for hot coffee can be partly attributed to cold weather. The habit of drinking large cups of boiled or filter-drip coffee with little or no milk also boosts consumption levels.

Although new to espresso, Nords also dominate the World Barista Championships (WBC). Beginning with the inaugural staging in 2000, six of the first seven annual competitions were won by Danes and Norwegians. The WBC Championship was created in Norway with a format based on the Norwegian Barista Championship, giving an edge to Norwegians and their neighbors.

According to the WBC's rigorous guidelines, each competitor must serve an espresso, a cappuccino, and a signature espresso-based beverage to four sensory judges, who evaluate them for appearance, accessories, taste balance, and quality. Two technical judges score for grinder usage, dosing and tamping consistency, extraction procedure, milk frothing, and hygiene.

The format does not appear to suit competitors from the nation former champion Fritz Storm of Denmark describes as "by far the best espresso-making country in the world": In the WBC's first eight years, not a single Italian placed first, second, or third. Upstarts from cultures where espresso is a recent phenomenon may have an advantage over Italian baristas with espresso in their veins. "They learn from a parent or an uncle," reasons Storm. "They are not studying like we are."

The Moka Pot
Stovetop Espresso in Every Italian Home

METAL CRAFTSMAN Alfonso Bialetti experienced his eureka moment while watching his wife do the laundry. Like most women of Crusinallo, Italy, she did her washing in a special metal pail heated over a stove. As the soapy water reached a boil, the pressure would push it up through a central tube only to sprinkle back down over the laundry. Bialetti imagined this washtub in miniature, with freshly brewed espresso flowing down from its center tube. He developed a two-chambered aluminum prototype: As water was heated to a boil in its lower vessel, steam pressure would force hot water up through a funnel-shaped basket of coffee grounds, pushing intensely flavored coffee up through a center nozzle, only to trickle down and collect in the upper chamber. Aromatic fumes would be released through its pouring spout, rousing all within the same walls from their morning slumber.

With his 1933 invention, Bialetti realized his goal—and every Italian's dream—of *in casa un espresso come al bar*—"an espresso in the home just like one in the bar." The Moka Express's ease of use and distinctive Art Deco outline, with octagonal upper and lower chambers tapering gently inward toward their meeting point, made it an icon of Italian design. Refinements and variations notwithstanding, the mechanism is fundamentally unchanged some seventy-five years later.

Today, the pot's cast-aluminum components are lined up by the thousands on a series of conveyer belts at the Bialetti plant in the northern Italian town of Omegna, known for its houseware foundries. One might think the survival of a nation depended on their production: 2.8 million units bearing Bialetti's "little man with a mustache" logo are packed there annually. An estimated nine of ten families in Italy have at least one Bialetti in their home.

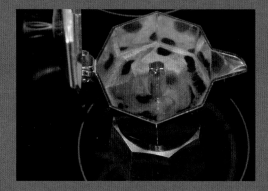

MOKA POT ESPRESSO

MAKES 1 SERVING • The espresso brewed in a moka pot can have a burnt, bitter quality. While millions of Italians might find that taste normal, it can mask a blend's aromatic character. To prevent the burning or "overcooking" of the coffee infusion as it accumulates in the upper chamber, simply leave the lid of the pot open as it brews.

Note: Moka pots are designed for a set number of small cups or servings. The size of the pot will determine how much coffee and water you need to use.

> 1 rounded tablespoon (about 7 grams) medium-fine
> ground coffee per serving (see note above)

Warm the entire pot by rinsing it in hot water. Dry the pot.

Remove the filter basket from the lower chamber of the pot and fill the lower chamber with cold water up to but not over the safety valve, about ⅓ cup per serving.

Replace the filter and fill it to the brim with coffee (about 1 rounded tablespoon per serving), gently leveling the grinds with your fingers so that the coffee is evenly distributed. Do not tamp or pack down the coffee.

Firmly screw the top section onto the base and place the pot over the burner. Leave the top lid open and turn the heat to medium-low.

When the upper chamber is filled about halfway and the flow from the nozzle begins to sputter, turn off the heat, close the lid, and, if using an electric stove, take the pot off the burner. Wait until the chamber is full and the sputtering noises have stopped before pouring into an espresso cup or demitasse. Serve hot.

Whipped Cream on Top

You Say "Schlag" and I Say "Panna"

SCHLAG IS SHORT FOR *schlagobers*, which means "beaten cream" in German. *Panna* is Italian for "cream" and, in its coffee applications, "whipped cream." Call it what you will, the quality of your Viennese *Einspänner* or Italian *caffe con panna* will be influenced by the quality of the cream itself.

Seek out the freshest, finest cream you can afford, perhaps splurging for an organic product from a local creamery or dairy farm. Look for a cream with a fat content of 35 to 36 percent. And be sure to choose a heavy cream that is pasteurized but not ultrapasturized, as ultrapasteurized cream has less flavor and is not as easy to whip. Monitor the thickness of the cream as you're beating it, a task most effectively performed by periodically dipping an index finger first in the cream and then in your mouth. Whipped cream is best when prepared just before using.

Whipped Cream

Schlagobers or Panna

MAKES 2 CUPS

> 1 cup heavy cream, well chilled
>
> 1 to 2 tablespoons confectioners' sugar, optional
>
> ½ teaspoon vanilla extract, optional

Combine the ingredients in a large metal mixing bowl, cover, and refrigerate, along with the beater blades (or wire whisk), for at least 30 minutes.

Beat the cream just until soft peaks form.

ESPRESSO CON PANNA

MAKES 1 SERVING • The same as *caffè con panna* or *kaffee mit schlag*, essentially a single or double espresso topped with a dollop of whipped cream or *panna*. Fabulous on its own—the thick cream slowly sinking into the coffee (unless you get to it first)—the *espresso con panna* also serves as the basic format for the fancier specialty house coffees at some of Italy's better cafés. Elaborately accessorized with syrups, berries, and nuts, capped with bonnets of fluffy cream, and presented in decorative, often colored glasses, these drinks resemble parfait extravaganzas, only in miniature.

**1 rounded tablespoon (about 7 grams) ground coffee,
(fine grind for espresso, medium-fine grind for a moka pot),
preferably an espresso blend**

1 dollop Whipped Cream (page 32)

If using an espresso machine, put the coffee in the filter basket of the portafilter, tamp down with a tamper, and secure the portafilter in the brew head. Place an espresso cup directly under the brew head, turn on the brew switch, and brew for 22 to 28 seconds to yield 1 to 1½ ounces of espresso. If using a moka pot, remove the filter basket from the lower chamber and fill the lower chamber with cold water up to the safety valve. Replace the filter, fill with coffee, gently level the grinds, screw the top section firmly onto the base, and place the pot over the burner. Leave the top lid open and turn the heat to medium-low. When the upper chamber is filled about halfway and the flow from the nozzle begins to sputter, turn off the heat, wait until the chamber is full and the sputtering noises have stopped, and pour into an espresso cup.

Spoon the whipped cream over the espresso. Serve immediately.

CAFFÈ MAROCCHINO

MAKES 1 SERVING • Virtually unknown outside Italy, the *caffè marocchino* (pronounced ma-roh-KEE-noh), essentially a mini-cappuccino dusted with cocoa, is wildly stylish in Milan and very popular in much of northern Italy. As coffees elsewhere get bigger and brasher, the Italians are downsizing. Their cappuccino, though already smaller than foreign interpretations of it, is apparently not small enough, hence the marocchino.

> **1 rounded tablespoon (about 7 grams) finely ground coffee, preferably an espresso blend**
>
> **2 to 3 tablespoons cold milk (whole, 2%, or nonfat)**
>
> **Pinch of cocoa powder**

Warm up the espresso machine. Put the coffee in the filter basket of the portafilter, tamp down with a tamper, and secure the portafilter in the brew head. Place an espresso cup directly under the brew head, turn on the brew switch, and brew for 22 to 25 seconds to yield 1 ounce of espresso.

Press the steam switch and wait for the ready indicator to light up. Meanwhile, pour the milk into a small stainless steel pitcher. Angling the pitcher, submerge the tip of the steam wand just below the milk surface and turn on the steam switch. As the foam rises, gradually lower the pitcher so the tip of the wand remains just below the milk surface and continue to steam until the side of the pitcher becomes too hot to hold. Turn off the steam while still holding the tip of the wand under the milk surface.

Gently pour the frothed milk over the espresso. Sprinkle with the cocoa powder. Serve immediately.

CAFFÈ SHAKERATO

MAKES 1 SERVING • An espresso shaken with ice and strained into a cocktail glass, the frothy *caffè shakerato* is the picture of simplicity and icy elegance. By *shakerato* the Italians mean "shaken," the term deriving from a cocktail shaker. Black-tied baristas at fancy Italian cafes do whatever they can to dress up the drink in evening wear—blending in milk, flavored syrups, and liqueurs (most commonly Bailey's); or adorning the glass with lemon peels, chocolate swirls, crunchy cookies, gossamer cream, whatever. But the Greta Garbo of cold coffees begs to be left alone.

> 2 rounded tablespoons (about 15 grams) finely ground coffee, preferably an espresso blend
>
> Ice cubes
>
> Simple Syrup (page 85) to taste, optional

Warm up the espresso machine. Put the coffee in the double-sized filter basket of the portafilter, tamp down with a tamper, and secure the portafilter in the brew head. Place a brewing pitcher or other receptacle directly under the brew head, turn on the brew switch, and brew for 22 to 28 seconds to yield 3 ounces of espresso.

Fill a cocktail shaker halfway with ice cubes, pour the espresso over the ice, and add syrup if desired. Shake vigorously for 10 long seconds and strain into a martini glass or other cocktail glass. Serve immediately.

TIRAMISÙ COFFEE

MAKES 4 SERVINGS • Norwegian barista Tim Wendelboe developed this drinkable version of the espresso-flavored Italian pastry with colleague Morten Wennersgaard for the 2004 World Barista Championship in Trieste, Italy. Wendelboe won the competition, and his "Tiramisù alla Tim" was honored as "WBC Signature Drink of the Year."

Reserve excess Marsala syrup for other coffee drinks, such as Latte Macchiato (page 26).

MARSALA SYRUP

2½ cups Marsala (or substitute sherry)

1 cup plus 2 teaspoons sugar

2 medium egg yolks, at room temperature

1 teaspoon confectioners' sugar

4 ounces mascarpone cheese, at room temperature

2 tablespoons whole milk, at room temperature

4 rounded tablespoons (about 30 grams) finely ground coffee

1 ounce grated dark chocolate, preferably orange flavored

To prepare the Marsala syrup: Combine the Marsala and 1 cup of the sugar in a saucepan and bring just to a boil over medium heat. Reduce the heat to low and simmer for 30 to 45 minutes, until all of the alcohol and most of the liquid has evaporated and you're left with a thick syrup. Remove from the heat and let cool.

Combine the egg yolks, confectioners' sugar, and 2 tablespoons of the Marsala syrup in a bowl and beat with a balloon whisk until fluffy.

Thin the mascarpone with the whole milk. Fold the mascarpone mixture into the egg mixture and whisk until fluffy. Transfer to a pitcher with a narrow spout.

Warm up the espresso machine. Put 2 rounded tablespoons of the coffee in the double-sized filter basket of the portafilter, tamp down with a tamper, and secure the portafilter in the brew head. Place a brewing pitcher or other receptacle directly under the brew head, turn on the brew switch, and brew for 22 to 28 seconds to yield 2 to 3 ounces of espresso. Repeat with the remaining coffee.

Stir the remaining 2 teaspoons of sugar into the espresso, and pour an equal amount of the sweetened espresso into each of four martini glasses or other cocktail glasses. Gently pour a half-inch layer of mascarpone-and-egg mixture over the espresso in each glass. Garnish with grated chocolate. Serve immediately.

Manuel Terzi

The Espresso Maestro of Bologna

AT HIS BOUTIQUE COFFEE bar in the gastronomic capital of Italy, Manuel Terzi (see photo on page 13) does more than just indulge the coffee cognoscenti. He also swells their ranks. His quintet of ground-to-order, single-origin espressos opens eyes and noses. His signature coffee drinks excite even the most overstimulated Bolognese palates. And his printed guarantee of a minimum dose of 7.5 grams of coffee per espresso shot, framed in gold and prominently displayed, hints at the integrity and precision of a craftsman who, by these measures, might be the greatest barista in Italy.

Terzi performs on a Faema E61 espresso machine, with solo and ensemble compositions assembled from five Mazzer Jolly burr grinders. He loads their conical hoppers with roasted coffee beans from five distinct growing regions, which itself is not unusual. Many coffee shops carry single-origin coffees chosen by a coffee selector who, like Terzi, knows every detail of their pedigrees. But most can only flirt with the idea of pulling single-origin espressos in addition to a mixed-origin house blend, just as cocktail bars have done with single-malt Scotches. They lack the equipment, the sure-handed baristas, or the willing, espresso-centric customers to pull it off.

Terzi takes espresso requests according to origin (India Plantation Bababudan might be one) or characteristic (such as low acidity), drawing a dose of 7.6 to 7.7 grams from the corresponding grinder. He also assembles custom blends on demand, collecting varying quantities from two or more grinders with the sure hands and staccato movements of an ace bartender mixing a signature cocktail.

Terzi's signature "cocktails" are liquid pastries garnished with accessories from a kit of marzipan cookie crumbs, meringue crumbs, candied orange peel, *amaretti* cookies, and various nuts. Their refinement is in keeping not only with the Caffè Terzi, which opened in Bologna in 2002 and incorporating design flourishes from 100 years earlier, but also with the dapper, meticulous *Maestro dell'Espresso* himself.

AL BIANCO

MAKES 2 SERVINGS • Lifting *bianco* ("white") from *cioccolatto bianco*, Manuel Terzi named his "white-chocolate" winter warmer to play off the Italian expression *al banco*—"at the bar." At his café in Bologna you can take this layered *millefoglie* of maple syrup, toasted caramelized almonds, melted white chocolate, and espresso *al banco* or *al tavolino*—"at the table."

> 8 caramelized almonds (or substitute any candied nuts)
>
> 2 tablespoons maple syrup
>
> 1 ounce white chocolate, finely chopped
>
> 4 rounded tablespoons (about 30 grams) finely ground coffee, preferably an espresso blend

Warm up the espresso machine. Place 4 almonds in each of two conical glasses and cover with 1 tablespoon of maple syrup per glass.

Heat the white chocolate in the top of a double boiler, stirring with a wooden spoon, until melted and smooth.

Put 2 rounded tablespoons coffee in the double-sized filter basket of the portafilter, tamp down with a tamper, and secure the portafilter in the brew head. Place a brew pitcher or other receptacle under the brew head, turn on the brew switch, and brew for 22 to 28 seconds to yield 2 to 3 ounces of espresso. Repeat with the remaining coffee.

Divide the melted white chocolate equally between the two glasses, then gently pour half of the espresso into each glass. Serve immediately.

GRANITA DI CAFFÈ

MAKES 4 TO 6 SERVINGS (1 PINT) • The very iced coffee of Sicily almost looks drinkable when the *panna* (whipped cream) topping seeps into the crevices of the flaky shaved ice crystals as they melt. At the famous Caffè Tazza d'Oro in Rome, the *panna* is placed both atop and beneath each serving of *granita di caffè*, an ingenious response to a chronic drawback of desserts—and sometimes romances—where sweet, lighter-than-air beginnings can lead to cold disappointment. With *panna* at the bottom, the finish is as sweet and creamy as the start.

⅔ cup (about 60 grams) finely ground coffee, regular or decaffeinated, preferably an espresso blend

1 to 1½ cups Whipped Cream (page 32), optional

¾ cup Simple Syrup (page 85)

Warm up the espresso machine. Put 2 rounded tablespoons coffee in the double-sized filter basket of the portafilter, tamp down with a tamper, and secure the portafilter in the brew head. Place a brewing pitcher or other receptacle directly under the brew head, turn on the brew switch, and brew for 22 to 25 seconds to yield 2 to 2½ ounces of espresso. Repeat until you have 1 cup of espresso.

Combine the espresso and the syrup in a baking pan or baking dish (about 9 inches square) and let cool. Cover with foil or plastic wrap and freeze for 30 minutes. Using the prongs of a fork, scrape the ice crystals forming at the edges of the pan toward the center. Repeat this process every 30 minutes or so, until the granita is frozen into fluffy flakes, about 3 hours. Keep in the freezer for up to 2 days.

Before serving, scrape and fluff the granita again with a fork, breaking apart any small chunks. Spoon a dollop of whipped cream into each glass, spoon the granita over the whipped cream, and top the granita with more whipped cream. Serve immediately.

NATIONAL BREWS

FILTER-BREWED COFFEE

MAKES 1 SERVING • Filter-brewed coffee is a low-tech path to good and even world-class coffee, but care is needed in its preparation. Proper water temperature is essential to extracting the full flavor of the ground coffee. Keep it near but not actually at a boil, between 195 and 205°F (90 and 95°C). Filter brewing requires a double pour: The first watering swells and compacts the grinds in preparation for the longer second pour.

If choosing between disposable paper and reusable metal mesh filters, bear in mind that paper filters are better at holding back sediment, which is beneficial if your grinder is producing an uneven grind. But paper also holds back some desirable oils. Beware of "cup" sizes attached to both filters and coffeemakers: These are usually small serving sizes measuring 4 to 5 ounces rather than the standard 8 ounces it would take to fill a small mug.

> 1 cup cold water
>
> 3½ to 4½ tablespoons (about 20 to 25 grams) ground coffee (fine grind for a cone filter, medium grind for a flat-bottomed basket filter)

In a saucepan or a kettle, bring the water to a boil, remove from the heat, and let cool for about a minute. Meanwhile, place the coffee in the filter.

Gently pour just enough hot water over the coffee to moisten all the grinds. Wait 30 seconds, then slowly pour the remaining water into the filter in a gentle, circular motion. Wait until the dripping has stopped and pour into a cup or mug. Serve immediately.

Turkish or Arabic?

It Boils Down to the Same Thing

SINCE THE COFFEE STYLE widely recognized as "Turkish" originated on the Arabian peninsula, "Arabic coffee," "Arabian coffee," or "Qahwah Arabiya" might be more fitting terms for a brewing process practiced throughout Turkey, Greece, the Balkans, the Middle East, and North Africa. The diversity of names for the long-handled pot used to boil this coffee—ibrik, briki, kanaka, cezve, toorka, raqwa—does not alter the basic method: Water, finely ground coffee, and sugar are heated to a near boil one or more times. The frothy coffee—and everybody loves that froth!—is slowly poured into small cups and then left alone to give the grounds time to sink to the bottom.

The coffee beans were traditionally toasted over a charcoal or wood fire. Now, though, it is more common for people to buy roasted coffee sold according to cultural preferences: Greeks generally favor a light roast; Turks, a medium; the Lebanese, a caramel-black dark. Sugar dosage is less predictable. Whereas the Turks designate six levels of sweetness, ranging from very sweet to stark black, Bedouin coffee has no sugar at all. On special occasions, the Lebanese may measure the sweetness according to the mood: more sugar for weddings, no sugar on days of mourning. In his work Turkish Coffee in Greece, author Elias Petropoulos counted forty-five ways Greeks take their coffee. One variety calls for three spoons of coffee, six spoons of sugar, and lots and lots of bubbles. The spice most commonly added to the coffee is fragrant cardamom, either as whole seeds or ground. In Persian Gulf countries, a thinner, filtered brew of Arabic coffee called qahwah or kahva typically contains more cardamom than coffee. Other flavorings added to coffee in Arab countries include saffron, aniseed, cloves, rose water, orange blossom water, cinnamon, nutmeg, and black pepper.

The sludgy dregs left at the bottom of the cup may have something to say about your future. First, the cup is inverted over the saucer and left a few minutes to let the sediment dry and settle on the sides of the cup. Then the dreamlike shapes may be read as symbolic clues by someone either trained or naturally gifted in the ancient fortunetelling practice of tasseography.

TURKISH COFFEE

MAKES 1 SERVING • Tending to the foam is the key to Turkish coffee preparation. The surface layer of rich, dense, dark-brown foam is the mark of a proper cup. If you don't keep an eye on the heating *ibrik* (long-handled pot) at all times, the neglected froth may suddenly gush from the pot like lava from a volcano and make an ugly mess. To nurture and build the froth, Turks customarily boil the coffee three or even four times, removing it from the heat as it begins to bubble up and letting it settle and cool a bit before returning it to the heat for the next boil.

Although the term "boiling" is commonly used, you mustn't let the coffee reach a full boil, as this would overcook the coffee.

The grind must be extra fine—powdery enough to dissolve, yet just weighty enough to sink to the bottom of the cup. If brewing two or more cups, figure on 1 heaping teaspoon of ground coffee per 6 tablespoons water.

- 1½ teaspoons (about 3 grams) extra finely ground coffee
- 1 teaspoon sugar, or to taste
- 6 tablespoons cold water
- 1 tiny pinch ground cardamom, optional

Combine the ingredients in an *ibrik* or very small saucepan and mix well. Heat over low heat and watch carefully, waiting for the froth to form and then expand inward from around the sides to cover the surface. Just as the froth begins to bubble up, quickly remove the pot from the heat and let the froth settle. Return to the heat and repeat for a second, third, and even fourth boil.

Pour the coffee into a demitasse and allow to sit for a couple of minutes to let the grounds settle on the bottom. Do not stir. Serve immediately.

The French Press

Coffee Pot with a Piston

AS WITH FRENCH FRIES, French toast, and French kisses, the French press is called something other than that in France: *cafetière à piston* ("coffeepot with a piston"); *Melior,* for the French manufacturer who first fitted the press with stainless steel filters; or *Bodum,* after the Danish manufacturer that has sold over 100 million of these coffeemakers since 1974. In Britain the pot is known as a cafetière. Italians call it a *caffettiera a pressofiltro* or a *caffettiera a stantuffo* (coffeepot with, respectively, a filter press or a piston). Americans know it as a French press, press pot, or plunger pot.

The French press consists of a glass, clear plastic, or stainless steel cylinder and a snug-fitting plunger with a wire-mesh disk that acts as a filter. Coarse coffee grinds are placed on the bottom of the cylinder, and near-boiling water is poured over it. After the coffee has steeped in the hot water for four minutes, the plunger is pushed carefully down to the bottom, its filter trapping the spent coffee grounds but not the freshly brewed coffee.

With the water in constant contact with the coffee and no paper filter to remove volatile oils, the French press is able to capture virtually all the characteristics of a roast. Another advantage is that the manual process does not dictate quantities or ratios of coffee and water. You can prepare a brew as strong as you want (up to a point) without compromising quality. Start with a high-quality beans—perhaps a Kenyan coffee with clean, complex flavor and berry-tinged acidity—and you'll get a thick, dense, yet very nuanced cup of coffee topped with a rich, mahogany-colored froth.

FRENCH PRESS POT COFFEE

MAKES 1 SERVING

3½ to 4½ tablespoons (about 20 to 25 grams)
medium coarsely ground coffee

1¼ cups water

Rinse the pot with hot water, then empty and dry it. Put the coffee in the pot.

In a saucepan or a kettle, bring the water to a boil, remove from the heat, and let stand for about a minute to let the water cool to 195 to 205°F (90 to 95°C). Pour the water over the coffee grinds and stir with the handle of a wooden spoon. Replace the lid and let the coffee steep for 4 minutes.

Very carefully push the plunger down to the bottom of the cylinder, making sure to keep it level. (Otherwise, spent grounds may circumvent the filter.) Make sure the lid is in the pouring position, then pour into a cup or mug. Serve immediately.

Café au Lait

A French Tale of Coffee "Socks" and Bowls

THE FRENCH *CAFÉ AU LAIT* (pronounced cah-FAY-oh-LAY) is hardly the same as an Italian *caffèlatte,* even if that is pretty much what you get when you order a café au lait at cafés in France. The iconic symbol of *le petit déjeuner* (breakfast) takes the shape of a bowl, preferably a chipped keepsake that used to belong to *grand-maman.* She probably made café au lait by filtering ground coffee blended with chicory through a sack of cotton, sometimes a flannel one, called a *café chaussette* (coffee sock). She would wet the coffee grinds first with a little near-boiling water, letting them swell for a spell, before adding the remainder of the water. She would achieve the café au lait color by combining equal parts of pan-heated milk and brewed coffee (or a coffee and chicory blend). "French roast," a universal description for a dark roast, is something of a misnomer, a *faux ami.* The French generally prefer lighter shades than their Italian, Spanish, and Portuguese neighbors to the south. They do, however, like their filter coffee reasonably strong. A Frenchman would ridicule a weak brew as *jus de chaussette*—"sock juice." The use of chicory as a coffee cohabitant was a custom born of necessity, due to a scarcity of either coffee beans or the *francs* to buy them. Cultivated in the Mediterranean and sought for centuries as an economical alternative to coffee, chicory use blossomed in France in the early nineteenth century, after Napoleon's Continental Blockade and its British reprisal cut off most coffee imports.

The commercial espresso machine changed French café customs after World War II. As the *café express,* a French corruption in language—and, often, in taste—of *caffè espresso,* acquired popularity and panache, the *café crème,* prepared with steamed milk (never cream) and espresso, replaced the café au lait in the Parisian lexicon. The change in terminology was fitting, since you can't easily dunk a fluffy croissant or crusty toasted *tartine* (slice of buttered bread) inside the narrow circumference of a small coffee cup, nor can you warm your body and soul on frigid winter mornings by leaning your face over a demitasse. For the authentic café au lait French breakfast experience you need a steaming bowl that you can hold in cupped hands.

CAFÉ AU LAIT

MAKES 2 SERVINGS • The quantities given here yield enough café au lait to nearly fill two 12-ounce (360-ml) bowls. Whatever the size and number of bowls (or cups) you want to fill, let these proportions be your guide before making adjustments for personal taste:

- For every ¾ cup (6 ounces) of water you will need 4 to 4½ table-spoons of ground coffee—less if you're adding chicory. Keep in mind that chicory is stronger than coffee, so less of it is needed.

- Because some water is absorbed by the spent grounds left behind in a filter or a French press, the volume of filtered [continued on page 50]

coffee will be less than that of the water poured into the filter. As a result, you start with 10 to 20 percent less milk than water to prepare an evenly balanced café au lait.

> 1 teaspoon medium-ground roasted chicory, optional
>
> 7 to 8 tablespoons (40 to 45 grams) ground coffee (fine grind for a cone filter, medium grind for a flat-bottomed filter, medium-coarse grind for a French press), preferably a medium roast
>
> 1½ cups water
>
> 1¼ cups milk (whole, 2%, or nonfat)

Place the chicory and then the coffee in the filter of a drip coffeemaker or the pot of a French press. Heat the water to a near boil, 195 to 205°F (90 to 95°C). If using a manual drip coffeemaker, pour just enough water over the coffee to wet the grinds. Wait 30 seconds and pour the remaining water over the coffee. For a French press, pour near-boiling water over the coffee and chicory, stir, and cover. Let steep for 4 minutes, then carefully push the plunger down to the bottom of the cylinder, making sure to keep it level.

Heat the milk in a small saucepan over medium heat, making sure not to let it boil, and beat with a whisk until frothy.

Pouring the brewed coffee and hot milk simultaneously, divide them equally between two bowls. Serve immediately.

CAFÉ CON LECHE

MAKES 1 SERVING • In Latin America, *café con leche* (pronounced cah-FAY con LAY-chay) customs can vary from country to country and household to household. Yet it is usually a sweet, milky coffee made with up to two thirds hot milk per one third brewed dark roast. Though *café con leche* can be made with drip or French press methods, the moka pot yields a potent brew that cuts through all that milk. The addition of cinnamon is a Mexican preference. Cubans like to dunk *tostada* (buttered grilled bread) into their morning coffee.

> ⅓ to ½ cup milk (whole or 2 percent, or substitute a mixture of whole milk and sweetened condensed milk)
>
> 1 cinnamon stick, optional
>
> 1 rounded tablespoon (about 7 grams) ground coffee (medium-fine grind for moka pot or fine grind for espresso), preferably dark roast

Pour the milk into a saucepan, add the cinnamon, if desired, and bring to just below a boil over medium heat. Cover and keep warm.

Remove the filter basket from the lower chamber of a single-serving moka pot and fill the lower chamber with cold water up to the safety valve. Replace the filter and fill to the brim with coffee, gently leveling the grinds. Screw the top section firmly onto the base and place the pot on the burner. Leave the top lid open, and turn the heat to medium-low. When the upper chamber is filled about halfway and the flow from the nozzle begins to sputter, turn off the heat and close the lid. If using an espresso machine, put coffee in the filter basket of the portafilter, tamp down with a tamper, and secure the portafilter in the brew head. Place a brew pitcher or another receptacle directly under the brew head, turn on the brew switch, and brew for 22 to 28 seconds to yield 1 to 1½ ounces of espresso.

Pour the milk into a cup, and top with the espresso. Serve immediately.

CAFÉ DE OLLA

MAKES 4 SERVINGS • You might guess just from this recipe's quantity of *piloncillo*, an unrefined brown sugar pressed in a cone shape, that this Mexican spiced coffee known as *café de olla* (pronounced oh-ya) is traditionally served either as an after-dinner coffee or as a sweet morning companion for *churros* (strips of fried dough). Uninitiated diners at Oyamel Cocina Mexicana in Washington, D.C., must be warned that its *café de olla* is generously presweetened before they make the error of blindly adding more sugar to the brew. The name comes from the earthenware pot used to prepare it. The longer the coffee steeps in an *olla* or, for that matter, a saucepan, the richer the flavor.

> 4 ounces *piloncillo*, chopped (substitute ½ cup brown sugar plus 1½ teaspoons molasses)
>
> 1 2-inch piece cinnamon stick, preferably canela
>
> ½ teaspoon anise seeds
>
> 1 cup (about 90 grams) medium coarsely ground coffee, preferably dark roast

Combine the *piloncillo*, cinnamon, anise seeds, and 1 quart cold water in a large saucepan over medium heat to a boil, stirring well to dissolve all the sugar. Remove from the heat, stir in the ground coffee, cover, and let steep for 5 to 10 minutes.

Strain the coffee through a fine sieve into 4 coffee mugs and serve.

Vietnamese Coffee
The Slow Drip of the Hatted Filter Press

THE DISTINGUISHING CHARacteristic of Vietnamese coffee is its filter press, essentially a one-cup coffeemaker that sits over the cup or glass like a hat. This stainless steel apparatus consists of three parts—a filter-bottomed pot, an upper screen that acts as a press, and a lid. Freshly brewed coffee drips slowly down from the mini-press pot, making the drinker wait up to an excruciating 300 seconds for his or her caffeine fix.

That painful but ultimately divine delay demonstrates the benefit of the Vietnamese filter for one-cup brewing. The slow drip ensures that the coffee grinds steep in hot water long enough for their aroma and flavor to be fully extracted. If similarly small quantities of ground coffee and water were fed into a basic drip machine with a conventional paper filter, the brewing time would be too rapid, and much of the coffee's character would be left behind in the filter.

Another advantage of the Vietnamese filter press is that it can be—and traditionally is—brought to the table so that the drinker gets something even fresher than freshly brewed coffee, namely not-yet-brewed coffee. When a thick glass, rather than a ceramic cup, is placed under the filter, the drinker can observe the entire brewing process. As the black coffee's downward flow decelerates from a steady trickle to a few scattered droplets, the drinker may slip into a hypnotic state, as if his heartbeat had slowed to the pace of the drip. This lull allows the full taste and impact of the strong coffee to be felt in the decisive first sip.

The coffee itself tends to be dark-roasted and may be blended with roasted chicory root, a taste the Vietnamese acquired from their French colonizers. In both its hot and iced versions, Vietnamese filter coffee is typically mixed with sweetened condensed milk, another by-product of French domination. Its sweet, concentrated milkiness tames the harshness of the strong, dark-roasted coffee, adds the perception of creamy richness, and gives the brew a dessert-like appeal. Better still, stirring the white condensed milk into the black liquid produces groovy swirls and enhances the hypnotic effect initiated by the Vietnamese filter's achingly slow drip.

VIETNAMESE COFFEE

MAKES 1 SERVING • What makes this style Vietnamese is a single-cup filter press pot, which you can buy for a few dollars at Asian food markets or at such sites as www.quickspice.com and www.importfood.com. Beans from Vietnam are neither required nor suggested.

Vietnamese coffee (called *Ca Phe*) is strong, both from the quantity and the character of the dark-roasted coffee recommended for its preparation. A Vietnamese coffee shop is likely to use as much coffee as is suggested below, if not more. Often this is a 90 percent–10 percent blend of roasted coffee and roasted chicory.

For a better view, try to use a small heatproof glass or a glass cup. For a hotter brew, warm the glass by filling it with hot water first and emptying it immediately before placing it under the filter pot.

> 2 to 3 tablespoons sweetened condensed milk (optional)
>
> 2 rounded tablespoons (about 15 grams) medium-ground coffee, preferably dark roast or a dark roast blended with chicory
>
> ⅔ cup boiling water
>
> Sugar to taste, optional

If preparing with sweetened condensed milk, begin by pouring that milk into a small glass or a glass coffee cup.

Remove the lid from a Vietnamese coffee filter pot and screw off the upper screen. Place the filter pot over the glass or cup, add the coffee to the filter container, and tap the container so the grinds settle somewhat evenly on the bottom. Screw the upper screen tightly over the coffee.

Pour enough boiling water to rise just slightly over the upper screen and wait 20 seconds. Unscrew the upper screen two turns, add enough boiling to fill the filter container, replace the lid, and let the coffee slowly drip until the liquid has drained, 4 to 5 minutes.

Remove the lid first and place it, inverted, on the table or counter. Remove the filter and place it atop the lid, which acts as a protective coaster. If you're not using sweetened condensed milk, stir sugar into the coffee. If you have used condensed milk, stir with the coffee until fully blended. Serve hot.

VIETNAMESE ICED COFFEE

MAKES 1 SERVING • *Ca phe sua da* sounds exotic, until you realize these words signify nothing more than the three ingredients in this sensational iced coffee treat: "coffee, milk, ice." The *sua* in question is sweetened condensed milk, which transforms cold, strong coffee into something akin to a silky coffee milkshake minus the froth. Vietnamese iced coffee can be prepared black, as in *ca phe da,* which is more refreshing but far less amusing than the milky elixir.

> **2 to 3 tablespoons sweetened condensed milk**
>
> **2 rounded tablespoons (about 15 grams) medium-ground coffee, preferably dark roast or a dark roast mixed with chicory**
>
> **²⁄₃ cup boiling water**
>
> **Ice**

Pour the condensed milk into a small glass or a glass coffee cup or mug.

Remove the lid from a Vietnamese coffee filter pot and screw off the upper screen. Place the filter pot over the glass, add the coffee to the filter container, and tap the container so the grinds settle somewhat evenly on the bottom. Screw the upper screen tightly over the coffee.

Pour enough boiling water to rise just slightly over the upper screen and wait 20 seconds. Unscrew the upper screen two turns, add enough boiling water to fill the filter container, and replace the lid. Let the coffee slowly drip until the liquid has drained, 4 to 5 minutes.

Remove the lid first and place it, inverted, on the table or counter. Remove the filter and place it atop the lid, which acts as a protective coaster. If you have used condensed milk, stir with the coffee until fully blended. Pour into a tall glass filled with ice. Serve with a straw.

Thai Coffee
Steeping Coffee, Brewing Conversation

AT RAN KOPEE GOE LUNG (literally, "shop coffee brother Lung") in the small town of Yantakhao, Thailand, the locals observed a self-imposed silence as they slowly stirred their coffees, listening for the sound the small spoon made as it circled the tall glass. Idle chatter did not begin until the layers of condensed milk and black coffee dissolved into brown and tan swirls.

"Drinking coffee created a sense of social participation," recalls Arun Sampanthavivat, the grandson of the late Gialung (Brother Lung) Yee and the chef-proprietor of the acclaimed Arun's restaurant in Chicago. "The minute they began to stir up the coffee in their cups was the minute they started all sorts of conversation, mostly about their families, social events, politics, etcetera. Back then there was no TV. Most communication was done in a coffee shop or a barber shop."

Gialung Yee, who was of Chinese descent, roasted his green coffee beans for hours in a large wok until they turned a dark, toasty color. He ground the roasted beans manually and brewed them in a cotton or muslin filter bag fitted to a metal ring, just as Bangkok street vendors do today. *Tung dtom kaffee* is the Thai term for a "coffee sock," meaning any cloth sack used as a coffee filter. Similar brewing bags in Thailand, Cambodia, Laos, Malaysia, and parts of South America are employed in much the same way: The open sack or cloth is filled with ground coffee, steeped in a pot of hot water, and then lifted out, taking away the spent grounds and leaving behind the finished brew.

Thai *oleang* (sometimes spelled *oliang* or *olieng*) is not so much coffee per se as a blend of coffee and grains. Soybean, ground corn, sesame seed, and chicory are added to round out the typically strong, even harsh, dark-roasted coffee favored by Thais. The most common substitute for those mellowing grains is ground cardamom. The brewed *oleang* is sweetened with sugar and consumed either hot or iced, often beneath a floating layer of sweetened condensed milk. From there, the conversation is stirred.

THAI ICED COFFEE

MAKES 2 SERVINGS • To prepare Thai coffee in the traditional manner you can purchase a muslin filter bag at Southeast Asian markets or from on-line retailers such as www.importfood.com and www.templeofthai.com. Alternatively, you can use a French press (see page 46), or let the coffee grinds steep directly in a pot of not-quite-boiling water, passing the brew through any coffee filter to remove the spent coffee grounds.

> 4 cardamom pods (or substitute ½ teaspoon ground cardamom)
>
> ½ cup (about 45 grams) medium coarsely ground coffee
>
> 2 cups boiling water
>
> Sugar to taste
>
> Crushed ice
>
> ¼ to ⅓ cup sweetened condensed or evaporated milk (or substitute half-and-half or heavy cream)

Break open the cardamom pods and grind the tiny seeds to a powder with a spice grinder or a mortar and pestle.

Combine the ground cardamom and coffee in a filter bag, a French press, or directly in a small pot. If using a filter bag, let it hang down into a small pot, carafe, or other receptacle. Pour boiling water over the coffee and cardamom and let steep for 10 minutes, then lift the filter bag out of the brew. If using a French press, stir, cover, and let steep for 10 minutes, then carefully push the plunger down to the bottom of the cylinder, making sure to keep it level. If using only a small pot, let the ground cardamom and coffee grinds steep directly in the water for 10 minutes, then pour the brew through a coffee filter or a sieve lined with cheesecloth.

Stir sugar (not too much if you're using sweetened condensed milk) into the filtered coffee. Divide the coffee equally between two tall glasses filled with ice. Hold a spoon over the coffee in the first glass, and gently pour the sweetened condensed milk over the spoon so that it floats in a sensuous layer at the top of the glass. Repeat with the second glass.

COLD-BREWED ICED COFFEE

MAKES 4 SERVINGS · The bitterness and staleness associated with iced coffees, especially when made from refrigerated hot coffee or hot coffee diluted with ice, is eliminated through "cold-brewing." You don't actually need to heat water to brew coffee, but you do need time: It can take up to twelve hours of cold-brewing to yield the proper strength of coffee solution. Cold-brewing proves to be a selective method, extracting and highlighting most of the desirable flavors in a coffee while leaving much of the bitterness and acidity behind. (These characteristics might be missed in a hot coffee but are less so in an iced one.) This recipe yields a coffee concentrate that should be diluted with an equal quantity of water or water and milk. You may prepare the solution in larger batches and store it for several days in the refrigerator.

2/3 cup (about 60 grams) coarsely ground coffee

3 cups cold water (preferably filtered water)

Simple Syrup (page 85) to taste, optional

Milk to taste, optional

Combine the coffee and water in a large jar, glass container, or French press, stir well, and cover. Let sit at room temperature for at least 6 hours and up to 12 hours.

To strain the coffee mixture, pour twice through a paper or mesh coffee filter, a Vietnamese coffee filter, or a sieve lined with cheesecloth; or push down the plunger of the French press. Refrigerate until ready to use.

To serve, combine the coffee concentrate with an equal quantity of cold water. Fill a tall glass halfway with ice, add the coffee solution and simple syrup, if using, and stir well. Top off the glass with a splash of milk, if desired. Repeat for each additional serving. Serve immediately.

COFFEEHOUSE
CULTURE

A Venetian Coffee Legacy

Primo Cameriere at the Piazza San Marco

MICHELE SIMIONATO WAS not raised to take up the family trade, as was his Venetian birthright. "A mother," he sympathizes, "wants better for her son." His father toiled as a waiter at Venice's venerable Caffè Florian, braving periodic inundations of water, pigeons, and tour groups in the Piazza San Marco so the young Michele could pursue his studies. Fate intervened. In 1975, Michele, then seventeen, accepted a summer job at the Florian and saw only opportunity. Were he to stay and pay his dues as a "second waiter," safely completing a million or so round trips from the interior service counter to the piazza tables without breaking too many cups, glasses, or limbs, he might one day don the black bowtie and lettered badge of a *primo cameriere*. The "first waiter" does not merely take orders from patrons: He must satisfy their every request with consummate skill. Ask him a question about the history of Venice, and he will deliver a spoken serenade: "In the middle of the sixteenth century, Venice was the center of the world . . ." Hand him a camera, and he will frame a portrait so flattering as to make an insurance adjuster from Tampa look as debonair as former Florian habitué Giacomo Casanova.

The Venezia Trionfante was opened beneath the arcades of the Procuratie Nuove in 1720 and soon after acquired the name of its owner, Floriano Francesconi. Dickens, Proust, Goethe, Byron, and many a literary luminary since has arranged to meet at "Florian's" for coffee, if not *the* coffee: It's doubtful anyone goes solely to sample the Venezia 1720, an adequate house blend of arabicas from Brazil and Costa Rica. Patrons gather either to luxuriate in the baroque splendor of the tearooms or to sit out with the masses on the magnificent piazza, where the Venezia 1720 can taste like the finest coffee in the world. During brief lulls, even Michele Simionato, who was promoted to *primo cameriere* in 1984, appears spellbound by the surroundings, as if glimpsing anew the domes of the Basilica. He would do well to watch his back instead. The snickering second waiters will be recording his every slip, as they do those of all their graying colleagues, wishing for— if not actually instigating—his retirement and, with it, another coveted opening for *primo cameriere*.

CAFFÈ IMPERATORE

MAKES 2 SERVINGS • The "emperor's coffee" is a specialty of the famous Caffè Florian. The foundation of this tricolored fancy is the Italian custard zabaglione, which originated in Venice back when its *imperatore* (pronounced eem-peh-rah-TOH-reh) ruled the Adriatic. You may substitute 3 ounces strong filtered coffee for the espresso.

2 large egg yolks, at room temperature

2 tablespoons sugar

2 tablespoons Marsala

2 rounded tablespoons (about 15 grams) finely ground coffee, preferably an espresso blend

Fresh Whipped Cream (page 32)

Warm up the espresso machine. To prepare the zabaglione: Combine the egg yolks and sugar in a bowl and beat with a balloon whisk until frothy. Gradually stir in the Marsala. Place the mixture in the top of a double boiler and beat continuously until thick, light, and foamy. Remove from the heat and continue to beat until the zabaglione has cooled.

Put the coffee in the double-sized filter basket of the portafilter, tamp down with a tamper, and secure the portafilter in the brew head. Place a brew pitcher or other receptable directly under the brew head, turn on the brew switch, and brew for 22 to 28 seconds to yield 3 ounces of espresso.

Divide the zabaglione between two heatproof glasses or goblets. Pour 1½ ounces of espresso over the zabaglione in each glass, then pour or spoon whipped cream on top. Serve immediately.

The Coffeehouse

Early Days of the Penny University

THE CAPACITY OF STUDENTS to drink large quantities of coffee, whether at a library to fuel their studies or at a coffeehouse to avoid them, is a centuries-old tradition. In 1587, the Arab scholar Abd al-Qadir al-Jaziri wrote about a Yemeni drink called *qahwa* used by Sufi *shaykhs* (mystical leaders) to help them stay awake at night, and by learned people seeking help in their studies. The Ottoman Turks took control of Yemen in the late 1530s and were soon exporting the prized beans from Mocha to the far reaches of their empire. Constantinople (now Istanbul), already home to Kiva Han, possibly the world's first coffeehouse (1471), quickly became the coffee capital of the world. By the early 1600s there were, according to scholar Ignatius Mouradgea d'Ohsson, six hundred coffeehouses in Constantinople. Arriving in 1610, Englishman George Sandys found men chatting all day long in "coffa-houses." He noted how they would "sippe of a drink called Coffa . . . in little China dishes, as hot as they can suffer it: blacke as soote, and tasting not much unlike it."

The first coffeehouse in London was founded in 1652 by Pasqua Rosee, an immigrant from Smyrna, Turkey. Within fifty years the English capital had, by historian Markman Ellis's estimate, four hundred to five hundred "penny universities," so nicknamed for the price of a coffee and the education that came with it. Ideas, knowledge, and opinions flowed freely. The networking and dealmaking helped transform a few coffeehouses into major trading centers. Edward Lloyd's Coffee House grew to become Lloyd's of London, the famous insurance market.

The appeal of coffee-fueled institutions of learning spread through Europe. Le Procope, the first café in Paris, debuted on the Left Bank in 1686. The literary landmark counted Voltaire, Balzac, Benjamin Franklin, Hugo, and Napoleon among its illustrious clientele. Venice's first *bottega del caffè* opened in the Piazza San Marco in 1683. Vienna, Prague, and Stockholm saw their first coffeehouses open in 1685, 1714, and 1718, respectively. The first license to sell coffee in Britain's American Colonies was granted to Dorothy Jones of Boston in 1670. Exactly 324 years later, that great city of higher learning got its first Starbucks.

CAFÉ LIÉGEOIS

MAKES 2 SERVINGS • A dessert classic from the grand cafés, brasseries, and music halls of Paris, the *café liégeois* (pronounced lee-ayje-wah) is what Americans would call a coffee float. Here's one instance in which you want to whip the heavy cream long and hard enough to form stiff peaks. In this way it can be decoratively piped from a pastry bag over the *café liégeois*. (If you don't have a pastry bag, spoon the whipped cream atop the glasses.)

> 6 tablespoons (about 35 grams) ground coffee (medium-fine grind for cone filter, medium grind for flat-bottomed filter, medium-coarse grind for French press), preferably medium roast
>
> 1½ cups water
>
> Fresh Whipped Cream (page 32), beat to stiff peaks (see note above)
>
> 1 tablespoon Simple Syrup (page 85), or to taste
>
> 2 large scoops coffee or vanilla ice cream
>
> 8 to 12 chocolate-covered coffee beans for garnish, optional

Place the coffee in the filter of a drip coffeemaker or the pot of a French press. Heat the water to a near boil (195 to 205°F/90 to 95°C). If using a manual drip coffeemaker, pour just enough of the water evenly over the coffee to wet the grinds. Wait 30 seconds, then pour the remaining water over the coffee. If using a French press, pour the water over the grinds, stir, and cover. Let steep for 4 minutes, then carefully push the plunger down to the bottom of the cylinder, making sure to keep it level. Let cool to room temperature, then refrigerate.

Load the whipped cream into a pastry bag and refrigerate until ready to use.

A minute before you're ready to serve, divide the cold coffee equally between two glasses and sweeten to taste with simple syrup. Place a scoop of ice cream in each glass and push it down into the coffee with a spoon.

Pipe the whipped cream over the glasses and garnish with the chocolate-covered coffee beans, if desired. Serve immediately.

The Vienna Coffeehouse

A Selection Like Nowhere Else

COFFEE AT THE VINTAGE coffeehouses of Vienna comes in innumerable shades of brown. Any customer may be as demanding as a Hapsburg prince, dithering among the near-blackness of a *Mokka* (a small, plain black coffee) or a *Verlängerter* (a *Mokka* diluted with water), the golden tint of the *Schale Gold* (a *Mokka* mixed with milk or cream), and various gradations in between. Within the tan-to-taupe realm are the *Brauner*, like a *Schale Gold* but slightly darker; the *Melange*, with equal parts *Mokka* and milk; and the *Kapuziner*, a cappuccino corrupted with whipped cream in place of milk foam. Standing apart in dark contrast is the *Einspänner*, a tall glass of black coffee crowned with a wealth of whipped cream.

Despite—or perhaps because of—the awesomeness of the selection, about three quarters of the Viennese habitués order a *Melange*. Although it has traditionally offered a greater variety of interesting coffees than nearly every other city, Vienna is pretty much a one-coffee town. Furthermore, the quality of the light- to medium-roast beans used in that coffee is variable. "Vienna did not have a coffee culture," notes Johanna Wechselberger, owner of a new-generation Viennese café, Mocca Club, and the Vienna School of Coffee. "It had a *Kaffeehauskultur*."

The Viennese could at least take pride in their great pastry culture. Even today, the dessert carts and windowed cases are the head-turners of the coffeehouse. Yet here, too, there is another rarely told tale. The diehard old-timers whose elegant dress and regal bearing uphold the grandeur of the *kaffeehaus* appear less concerned with the pastry selection than the newspaper selection. The famous billiards table at Café Sperl, perhaps the most authentic and least museumlike of the classic coffeehouses, is routinely covered with daily newspapers. The Sperl regulars, throwbacks who look like characters from a 1930s movie, devour the newspapers one by one, from morning to afternoon.

"I used to ask myself, 'What is the difference between the *konditorei* [patisserie] and the café?'" muses Hans Diglas, who runs exemplars of both under the Café Diglas name. "The café is less pastries and more newspapers."

MARIA THERESIA

MAKES 1 SERVING • Named after the Austrian empress who served as Queen of Hungary and Bohemia from 1740 to 1780, the Maria Theresia is an absolute must on the menus of old coffeehouses in Vienna, Prague, and Budapest. That isn't to suggest the baristas in those capitals get much practice preparing this classic; most young Viennese have never heard of it. When one is ordered, according to Hans Diglas of the Café Diglas in Vienna, it is invariably by an old-timer or a fortunate foreigner surrendering to the frivolous charms of a grander *époque*. The Maria Theresia is the sort of merry confection that begs to be accompanied by a Strauss waltz (such as "The Blue Danube"). You may substitute 3 ounces strong filtered coffee for the espresso.

> 2 rounded tablespoons (about 15 grams) finely ground coffee, preferably a light or medium roast
>
> 3 tablespoons orange liqueur
>
> 1 large dollop of lightly sweetened Whipped Cream (page 32)
>
> 1 teaspoon grated orange zest

Warm up the espresso machine. Warm a tall, stemmed dessert glass or glass mug by rinsing it with hot water. Empty and dry the glass.

Put the coffee in the double-sized filter basket of the portafilter, tamp down with a tamper, and secure the portafilter in the brew head. Place a brew pitcher or other receptacle directly under the brew head, turn on the brew switch, and brew for 22 to 28 seconds to yield 2 to 3 ounces of espresso.

Pour the orange liqueur in the prewarmed glass; top first with espresso, then with whipped cream. Sprinkle with grated orange zest and serve.

Tray, Coffee, Water, Sugar
Still Life at the Viennese Coffeehouse

THE POLISHED-METAL COF-fee tray is a Viennese landmark as worthy of preservation as the Thonet chairs, crystal chandeliers, and marble tables of the Café Sperl; the great vaulted ceiling and marble columns of the Café Central; or the Franz Hubmann photos on the dark-as-espresso wood walls of the Café Hawelka. As integral to the timeless still life of the Viennese coffeehouse as coffee, water, and sugar cubes, the tray is not an appendage of the waiter's palm, to be emptied of its contents and whisked away. Removing it from a coffee order would be like pulling a saucer out from under its cup.

In twenty-first-century Vienna, those sugar cubes perform the same sweetening function as granulated sugar in packets, canisters, or stick packs. But back in the days before espresso machines, when coffee was still boiled and filtered, the cubes also served as a unit of currency. Sugar was expensive, and cubes of it were as valuable as coins. Cashiers kept track of what waiters owed them by keeping count of the sugar cubes that accompanied their coffee orders. Each coffee drink was assigned a set number of cubes—three for a *Melange*, four for a double *Mokka*, and so on. Assuming a value of 1 shilling per sugar cube, the waiter would, at the end of his shift, owe the cashier 3 shillings for every *Melange* he had served that day and for which he had collected payment directly from the customer, in cash. No other commodity was accepted from customers, the notable exception being the artwork occasionally offered as payment by Bohemian patrons at the Café Hawelka. Electromechanical cash registers introduced in the 1950s and 1960s spurred the demise of sugar-cube tabulation but fortunately not of the cubes themselves, nor of the polished-metal trays atop which this sweet currency changed hands.

EINSPÄNNER

MAKES 2 SERVINGS • The knowledge that *Einspänner* is a term for a one-horse carriage offers few clues but inspires many theories as to the Viennese coffee's origins. The best I can do is imagine that there was a tall guy named Einspänner who wore a fluffy white wig and a long black cloak and drove a coach around town and drank coffee. No matter. The stretched counterpart to the Italian *caffè con panna* is a classic made only with contrasting essentials of the dessert coffee genre: black coffee and whipped cream. The quantity of the latter can be adjusted to counter the resistance of dieters who scream when they hear the word "cream."

½ cup (about 45 grams) ground coffee (medium-fine grind for cone filter, medium grind for flat-bottomed filter, medium-coarse grind for French press), preferably light or medium roast

2 cups water

Fresh Whipped Cream (page 32)

Place the coffee in the filter of a drip coffeemaker or the pot of a French press. Heat the water to a near boil (195 to 205°F/90 to 95°C). If using a manual drip coffeemaker, pour just enough of the water evenly over the coffee to wet the grinds. Wait 30 seconds, then pour the remaining water over the coffee. If using a French press, pour the water over the grinds, stir, and cover. Let steep for 4 minutes, then carefully push the plunger down to the bottom of the cylinder, making sure to keep it level.

Divide the coffee equally between two tall, heatproof glasses (put a spoon in each if you're unsure). Place a spoon over each glass and pour whipped cream over the spoon to form a layer no thinner than 2 inches. Serve immediately.

MELANGE

MAKES 2 SERVINGS • The *Melange*—German for "blend"—has nothing to do with the coffee blends sold as Viennese roast, which paradoxically are too dark and bitter for the Viennese palate. Rather, *Melange* indicates the classic, 50–50 mix of hot milk and coffee (from a light-to-medium roast) that is Vienna's favorite shade of brown. When an espresso machine is used to prepare a *Melange,* the classic formula is adjusted to the 1:2 espresso-to-milk ratio of an Italian cappuccino, only with much less froth. If you're using the steam wand of an espresso machine, take care not to suck too much air into the milk.

> **5 to 6 tablespoons (about 28 to 34 grams) ground coffee (medium-fine grind for cone filter, medium grind for flat-bottomed filter), light or medium roast**
>
> **1¼ cups water**
>
> **1 cup milk (whole, 2%, or nonfat)**

Place the coffee in the filter of a drip coffeemaker. If using a manual drip coffeemaker, heat the water to a near boil (195 to 205°F/90 to 95°C). Pour just enough of the water evenly over the coffee to wet the grinds. Wait 30 seconds, then pour the remaining water over the coffee.

Heat the milk in a small saucepan over medium heat, making sure not to let it boil, and beat with a whisk until frothy.

Divide the coffee equally between two cups. Top with the hot milk. Serve immediately.

The Gresham Kávéház
Jamaican Coffee on the Danube

BUDAPEST'S GRESHAM Palace, an Art Nouveau treasure perfectly positioned on the banks of the Danube, was nearly destroyed by Nazi bombing and Communist neglect. The famed Chain Bridge connecting Buda to Pest practically points at its main entrance. To restore the Gresham's magnificent facade and install a Four Seasons Hotel beneath it, master craftsmen from all over Europe were brought in to re-create the palace's spectacular mosaics, ironwork, and glasswork. Naturally there had to be a café, inspired by the great coffeehouses of Budapest and reminiscent of the Gresham-Venezia, a favorite haunt of the Hungarian intelligentsia many years ago. The hotel and its Gresham Kávéház opened in 2004.

The Kávéház is at all times beautiful and sometimes busy. But were it not for the sensational view, you could be at any number of luxurious hotel coffee shops. Something extra was needed to honor the city's great coffeehouse tradition. Strangely, that addition turned out to be an espresso priced at 1,900 Hungarian forint (roughly $12.25), not normally the sort of thing to attract near-starving artists and Bohemians. The espresso is pulled from exorbitantly priced Jamaica Blue Mountain beans—roasted on demand, if the customer so desires, in a machine no bigger than a home drip coffeemaker. Unfortunately, the home roaster stays home, in the café's kitchen, so the customer does not get to see and smell the beans as they roast.

The espresso, expertly ground, tamped, and pulled by one of the Gresham's sure-handed baristas, is rich, aromatic, and overpriced. The Jamaican Blue Mountain was likely chosen for its rarity and a long-standing reputation as the best coffee in the world, whether or not that label still qualifies (although it may still be one of the best). The roasting on demand may add an intolerable ten minutes to the wait for a coffee, but it is a wonderfully silly extravagance far more affordable than, say, an Hermès bag. The mere fact that the Gresham is offering the service speaks to the newfound cachet of coffee. Back when palaces like this were still palaces, vintage Champagne and Tokaji wine were the status drinks. Now, roasted-to-order coffee joins their ranks.

BICERIN

MAKES 2 SERVINGS • *Bicerin* (pronounced bee-chay-reen) means "small glass" in Piedmontese, a dialect understood in Turin, Italy, where the regionally famous drink by that name is a three-layered coffee of hot chocolate, sweetened espresso, and cream served, ironically, in a not-so-small glass (see cover photo). There is, however, considerable disagreement among the Torinese as to the order of the lower and middle layers and the consistency of the top one. Some pour the hot chocolate in the bottom of the glass and cover it with a band of espresso, while others do the reverse. And while many beat their cream before laying it atop the glass, the practice is disparaged as a sham by the landmark Caffè al Bicerin, a resident of the Piazza della Consolata since 1763. (For the record, they pour in the espresso first.) I've sampled several bicerin examples in Turin and tested several permutations at home and have concluded that the superiority of Caffè al Bicerin's espresso-first interpretation has less to do with its all-liquid layering than the quality of its legendary homemade *cioccolata*. Of course I could be rationalizing: It's just much easier to succeed at floating the cream on top by adding the espresso second and, more importantly, whipping the cream to stiffen it just a little.

⅔ cup whole milk

2½ ounces (about 70 grams) bittersweet chocolate, chopped or shaved

4 rounded tablespoons (about 30 grams) ground coffee (fine grind for espresso, medium-fine grind for a moka pot), preferably an espresso roast

Sugar to taste, optional

½ cup Whipped Cream (page 32), not beaten too stiffly

Heat the milk in a small saucepan over medium heat to a simmer, stir-ring occasionally with a whisk. Add the chocolate and heat, whisking con-stantly, until the chocolate is melted and smooth. Simmer for another minute and then remove from the heat.

If using an espresso machine, put 2 rounded tablespoons coffee in the double-sized filter basket of the portafilter, tamp down with a tamper, and secure the portafilter in the brew head. Place a brew pitcher or other receptacle directly under the brew head, turn on the brew switch, and brew for 22 to 28 seconds to yield 3 ounces of espresso. Repeat with the remaining coffee grinds. If using a moka pot, remove the filter basket from the lower chamber and fill the lower chamber with cold water up to the safety valve. Replace the filter and fill with 1 rounded tablespoon for a single-serving pot or 2 rounded tablespoons for a double-serving pot. Gently level the grinds, screw the top section firmly onto the base, and place the pot over the burner. Leave the top lid open and turn the heat to medium-low. When the upper chamber is filled about halfway and the flow from the nozzle begins to sputter, turn off the heat and wait until the chamber is full and the sputtering noises have stopped. Repeat with the remaining coffee grinds. Sweeten the coffee with sugar to taste.

Divide the hot chocolate equally between two heatproof glasses, pour the espresso over the chocolate, place a spoon over the glass, and pour the whipped cream over the spoon to fill the glass. Serve immediately.

ESPRESSO PEPPERINO

MAKES 1 SERVING · I was a little disappointed when I first tried the *esz-presszó csokoládéval és borssal* at the Central Kávéház. I had no complaint with the café itself, which, though rebuilt in 2000 inside its circa-1887 former self, has the authentic feel and vitality of Budapest's classic coffeehouses. But I was hoping the *pepperino* would be dusted with red Hungarian paprika, a great foil for chocolate and possibly also for coffee. It came instead with black pepper applied by the waiter from a table shaker. The pepper wasn't even freshly ground! I tried making *pepperino*

at home with a medium-hot paprika and it's terrific, though better with a little sugar in the espresso. You need espresso with *crema* so the cocoa and pepper powder float on the surface, rather than sinking to the bottom. The dusting also works for a cappuccino.

> 1 rounded tablespoon (about 7 grams) finely ground coffee, preferably an espresso roast
>
> 1 small pinch cocoa powder
>
> 1 very small pinch ground paprika, preferably medium-hot

Warm up the espresso machine. Put the coffee in the filter basket of the portafilter, tamp down with a tamper, and secure the portafilter in the brew head. Place an espresso cup or demitasse directly under the brew head, turn on the brew switch, and brew for 22 to 28 seconds to yield 1 to 1½ ounces of espresso.

Sprinkle with the cocoa and paprika and serve immediately.

COFFEE MILKS
AND SHAKES

COFFEE MILKSHAKE

MAKES 1 SERVING • When Rob Fischer, owner of the Palo Alto Creamery (aka The Creamery) in Palo Alto, California, says the secret to his diner's famous milkshakes is consistency, he is referring to their dependability, not their density or texture. Yet it is the consistency of their consistency—their reliably thick-but-not-too-thick texture—that is paramount. For that, Fischer swears by a 2:1 ice cream–to-milk ratio. He advises against super-premium ice cream such as Häagen-Dazs. "The fat," he says, "ends up coating the palate and you can't taste the flavor." He prefers a premium ice cream with a butterfat content of about 12 percent. At The Creamery he uses Treat, a local ice cream from San Jose.

The flavor in coffee ice cream is not strong enough to carry the milkshake—you need to add coffee syrup to sweeten it. For greater intensity of coffee flavor, add a shot of espresso.

> 2 cups coffee ice cream
> 1 cup whole milk, as cold as possible
> 2 tablespoons Coffee Syrup (page 93)

Combine all ingredients in a blender and blend until smooth. Pour into a tall glass and serve with a straw.

MOCHA MILKSHAKE

MAKES 1 SERVING • The mocha is a great combination milkshake when coffee ice cream is matched to chocolate syrup, but not as good when the flavors are switched. Try it yourself.

> **2 cups coffee ice cream**
>
> **1 cup milk, as cold as possible**
>
> **2 to 3 tablespoons chocolate syrup**

Combine all ingredients in a blender and blend until smooth. Pour into a tall glass and serve with a straw.

RHODE ISLAND COFFEE MILK

MAKES 1 SERVING • Named the official state drink of Rhode Island in 1993, coffee milk is comparable to chocolate milk, except that coffee syrup is used in place of chocolate syrup. Little known in the big world outside the smallest state, coffee milk may have been introduced or at least popularized by Italian immigrants. It became a popular refreshment in the 1930s at Rhode Island diners, drugstore soda fountains, and ice cream parlors and to this day is typically prepared with one of two local brands of coffee syrup from that era: Eclipse ("you'll smack your lips if it's an Eclipse") and Autocrat ("A swallow will tell you").

Autocrat, the sweeter of the two, outsells Eclipse, which is stronger in coffee flavor. A third brand, Coffee Time, has still more coffee power. You can do your own comparison (bottles are sold online at www.autocrat.com and www.hometownfavorites.com).

1 cup milk

2 to 3 tablespoons Coffee Syrup (page 93)

Pour the milk in a glass, add the coffee syrup, and stir well. Serve immediately.

COFFEE ICE CREAM SODA

MAKES 1 SERVING • Ice cream sodas taste better when milk is added to the syrup-flavored soda. Using melted vanilla ice cream instead of milk multiplies that milky–creamy effect tenfold. It was suggested by the Palo Alto Creamery, and it's a devilish idea: Since life is short, why wait for the ice cream to melt into the soda when you can achieve this effect from the get-go? You can substitute coffee ice cream to increase the coffee intensity or to avoid having to buy two ice cream flavors. In a pinch, you can always just use milk and still end up with a great ice cream soda, if not quite the same transformational experience.

> 3 tablespoons Coffee Syrup (page 93)
>
> ¼ cup vanilla ice cream, fully melted (or substitute cold whole milk)
>
> 1 to 1½ cups soda or seltzer water
>
> 1 large scoop coffee ice cream

Pour the syrup into a tall glass, add the vanilla ice cream, and stir. Pour in the seltzer, continuing to stir the drink, to within 2 inches of the top of the glass.

Add the scoop of coffee ice cream, preferably making it big enough to just fit the circumference of the glass, and try to leave it straddling the rim of the glass for effect. Serve immediately.

The Simple Solution

Syrup Instead of Sugar

T IS A CHEMISTRY LESSON learned by iced tea and iced coffee drinkers alike: Granulated sugar does not dissolve in cold liquid. Agile drinkers seeking a uniformly sweet drink have resorted to stirring up the sugar at the bottom of the glass and angling the straw near—but not at—the bottom of the glass, so that only the right quantity of loosened grains are sucked up with each successive sip. The limits of this technique are made evident by the diminishing sweetness of the drink, or, more often and more plainly, the sugary sediment coating the bottom of the depleted glass.

Only fairly recently have coffee shops adopted a simple solution. A staple for pastry cooks and candy makers, a simple syrup (sometimes called sugar syrup, simple sugar syrup, bar syrup, or stock syrup) is prepared by heating a mixture of sugar and water until the sugar is fully dissolved and a clear syrup is formed. In baking and confectionery, the syrup is used for frosting, glazing, and soaking; for preserving or sweetening fruit; and as the basis for candies. For bartenders and baristas, simple syrup dissolves easily into cold drinks and is the starting point for most flavored syrups.

Simple syrup can be prepared in different densities, from thin (3 parts water per 1 part sugar) to thick (1 part water per 2 parts sugar). When used as a sweetener for coffee drinks, medium-thick syrup (equal parts water and sugar) is advised. That 1:1 ratio should be used in recipes in this book that call for simple syrup, unless the instructions state otherwise.

Manuel Terzi, an espresso virtuoso from Bologna, Italy, suggests using raw pure cane sugar, such as Demerara, or turbinado, which enhances the coffee flavor and aroma, whereas white sugar may impart subtle defects wrongly attributed to the coffee. The lower melting point of cane sugar is also beneficial when preparing syrup: You don't have to heat it as much.

SIMPLE SYRUP

1 cup granulated sugar
(white or pure unrefined cane)

1 cup water

Combine the sugar and water in a small saucepan over medium-high heat and simmer, stirring with a wooden spoon, until the sugar is completely dissolved and the syrup is clear. Remove from the heat and let cool.

Transfer to a clean lidded jar or, ideally, a syrup dispenser, and refrigerate for up to one month.

CAFÉ FRAPPÉ

MAKES 1 SERVING • This is the original frappé, once a centerpiece of the French brasserie's coffee and dessert repertoires. The name comes from the French verb *frapper*, which, though it means "to hit" or "to strike" (maybe like a frappé in a blender), indicates "iced" or "cold" in a beverage context. The classic frappé is in most instances thinner than an American milkshake, which, confusingly, is called a "frappe" (pronounced "trap," not "fra-PAY") in Boston. In Italy a *frappè al caffè* is a blend of espresso, sugar or syrup, crushed ice, and sometimes vanilla extract. Feel free to add your favorite flavored syrup or liqueur, as the brasserie mixologist certainly would.

2 rounded tablespoons (about 15 grams) ground coffee (fine grind for espresso, medium-fine grind for cone filter, medium grind for flat-bottomed filter, medium-coarse grind for French press)

¾ cup water, if using a manual drip coffeemaker or French press

½ cup sweetened condensed milk

1 small scoop vanilla ice cream

A few drops vanilla extract, optional

3 ice cubes, crushed

If using espresso, warm up the espresso machine. Put the coffee in the double-sized filter basket of the portafilter, tamp down with a tamper, and secure the portafilter in the brew head. Place a brew pitcher or other receptacle directly under the brew head, turn on the brew switch, and brew for 22 to 28 seconds to yield 3 ounces of espresso. If using a manual drip coffeemaker, pour just enough near-boiling water (195 to 205°F/ 90 to 95°C) over the coffee to wet the grinds. Wait 30 seconds, then pour the remaining water over the coffee. For a French press, pour the near-boiling water over the coffee, stir, and cover. Let steep for 4 minutes,

then carefully push the plunger down to the bottom of the cylinder, making sure to keep it level. Let the espresso or coffee cool to room temperature.

Combine the cooled coffee with the remaining ingredients in a blender and blend until smooth. Serve immediately with a straw.

The Greek-Style Frappé

In Praise of Foam

ACCORDING TO POPULAR legend, the Greek-style frappé was invented in September 1957 at the annual Thessaloniki International Trade Fair in the convention center of Greece's second-largest city. Working at an exhibit for Andreas Dritsas, then the Greek distributor of Nestlé products, sales rep Dimitrios Vakondios grabbed a shaker meant for Nesquik cocoa, filled it instead with Nescafé instant coffee and a little cold water, and shook it vigorously. Not anticipating the burst of foam this action would generate, Vakondios achieved two results: The first was the staining of his business suit; the second, the invention of the foamy concoction that would become something akin to the national soft drink of Greece.

The hallmark of the iced coffee Greeks call frappé is a thick head of microfoam. Its mystery comes from the fact that its frothiness is not produced by ice cream, blended ice, or thickening agents, as it is with Starbucks Frappuccino, French-style frappé, or other frothy cold coffees. Even when prepared black without a splash of milk (typically evaporated milk), the Greek frappé holds its microbubbled head high.

Many Athenians have suspected that Lentzos, a 1970s café in the city's Pangrati district, added beaten egg whites to its frappés to make their foam meringue-like. But it's a myth: Coffee foams, such as espresso *crema*, are created by proteins that act as surfactants (surface active agents), forming a thin elastic membrane on the liquid's surface area and entrapping air. The main advantage instant coffee has over brewed fresh coffee for the purpose of foaming is that it can be prepared in a highly concentrated solution. When that solution is shaken, there are lots of proteins to line the bubbles that form and help produce a thick, durable foam. Water and milk can then be added to fill the glass.

Frappé foam can last for hours, and due to the modern Greek's drawn-out drinking habits, often does. The liquid level in the Greek's frappé glass seems to set more slowly than the Aegean sun. As the foam eventually recedes, puffy peaks hover fuzzily above the liquidlike mountains over the sea. Below that ethereal cloud is a rich refreshment that looks like a coffee milkshake yet glides easily through the narrowest of straws.

GREEK-STYLE FRAPPÉ

MAKES 1 SERVING • For Greeks who live by this sensationally frothy iced coffee and non-Greek initiates who swear by it, the way they drink their frappé—one, two, or more teaspoons (level, rounded, or heaping) of coffee; with milk or black; unsweetened, medium-sweet, or super-sugary—is a matter of personal expression. Setting down specific quantities for its preparation therefore contradicts the frappé spirit. The amounts suggested below are best used only as a departure point; adjustments should then be made according to personal taste and mood.

2 teaspoons instant coffee

2 teaspoons sugar

Cold water

Ice cubes

2 tablespoons evaporated or regular milk, optional

Place the coffee, sugar, and 2 tablespoons cold water in a shaker, jar, blender, or drink mixer. Cover and shake well for 30 seconds, or, if using a blender, drink mixer, or handheld frother, mix for 15 seconds to produce a thick, light-brown foam.

Place a few ice cubes in a tall glass. Slowly pour the coffee foam into the glass. Fill the glass with water, adding milk if desired. Serve immediately with a thin, flexible straw and glass of cold water on the side.

CAFFÈ FREDDO

MAKES 1 SERVING • The Italians often top *freddo*, their iced espresso, with blended milk that is thick and fluffy enough to float on the surface. The Greeks, who love their interpretation made with evaporated milk, think of it as an Italian classic. Yet the Greek version of *freddo* rarely fails to wow visiting Italians. "Amazing!" said a barista from Venice's Caffè del Doge. "We can't do anything like that." You can use the same milk topping for a cold-brewed iced coffee (page 60).

> 2 rounded tablespoons (about 15 grams) finely ground coffee, preferably an espresso roast
>
> Simple Syrup (page 85) to taste
>
> Ice cubes
>
> 3 tablespoons evaporated or whole milk, optional

Warm up the espresso machine. Put the coffee in the double-sized filter basket of the portafilter, tamp down with a tamper, and secure the portafilter in the brew head. Place a brew pitcher or other receptacle under the brew head. Turn on the brew switch and brew for 22 to 28 seconds to yield 3 ounces of espresso.

Combine the espresso and syrup in a shaker, fill with ice, and shake vigorously. Strain into a chilled cocktail glass.

If adding a milk topping, pour the milk in a blender and blend until thickened. Place a spoon over the glass and slowly pour the beaten milk over the spoon. Serve immediately.

Coffee Syrup
Getting Into the Thick of It

THE BIGGEST OBSTACLE TO preparing a homemade coffee syrup is devising a sufficiently concentrated coffee solution to flavor it. You essentially want a double- or even triple-strength coffee, which is not as easy to achieve as it may seem. Using a standard drip coffeemaker or espresso machine, you can't simply double the amount of ground coffee for the same amount of water, as this would clog the filter, over-extract the coffee, and produce a bitter taste. Some syrup recipes call for recycling the coffee liquid—first brewing a standard-strength pot of filter coffee and using it, rather than fresh water, to brew a progressively stronger second and third pot. But the result can be harsh on your syrup and hard on your coffeemaker.

The simplest alternative is to use instant coffee, which is manufactured by removing the moisture from coffee that has already been roasted, ground, and brewed. You can fashion a progressively stronger liquid extract by decreasing the water quantity you would typically add to a given amount of instant coffee. The drawback with using instant coffee is its processed taste.

If you want your syrup to taste like your favorite coffee—admittedly an elusive goal, considering how much sugar you will be adding—there are two ways to achieve the desired coffee strength without spoiling the flavor:

- Use an espresso machine, pulling a series of short, ⅔-ounce shots— what the Italians call *caffè ristretto* or simply *ristretto* ("restricted").

- Cold-brew the coffee, letting the grinds steep in a relatively small quantity of cold water for several hours.

The syrup made from cold-brewed coffee is a great all-purpose syrup and a superb dessert topping for ice cream or yogurt. The espresso syrup is richer and more complex, with a bright aftertaste. The first coffee milk (page 82) I made with it was so good I was tempted to go into the espresso syrup business.

COLD-BREWED COFFEE SYRUP

MAKES 1 TO 1¼ CUPS

⅓ cup (about 30 grams) coarsely ground coffee

1¼ cups cold water (preferably filtered water)

1 cup sugar

Combine the coffee and water in a large jar, glass container, or French press, stir well, and cover. Let sit at room temperature for at least 6 hours and up to 12 hours.

To strain the coffee mixture, pour twice through a paper or mesh coffee filter, a Vietnamese coffee filter, or a sieve lined with cheesecloth; or push down the plunger of the French press.

Combine the coffee and the sugar in a saucepan over medium-high heat and heat, stirring with a whisk, to just below a boil. Lower the heat to moderately low and simmer, stirring, until the mixture begins to thicken and its volume has been reduced by a quarter for thinner syrup or a third for thicker syrup, about 7 to 10 minutes. Remove from the heat, let cool, cover tightly, and store in the refrigerator for up to 2 weeks.

ESPRESSO SYRUP

MAKES 1 TO 1¼ CUPS

1 cup (about 90 grams) finely ground coffee, preferably medium-dark or dark roast

1 cup sugar

Warm up the espresso machine. Put 2 rounded tablespoons of coffee in the double-sized filter basket of the portafilter, tamp down with a tamper, and secure the portafilter in the brew head. Place a brew pitcher or other receptacle directly under the brew head, turn on the brew switch, and brew for 15 to 20 seconds to yield about 1⅓ ounces of espresso. Repeat with the remaining coffee grinds to yield a total of 1 cup espresso.

Combine the espresso and the sugar in a saucepan over medium-high heat and heat, stirring with a whisk, to just below a boil. Lower the heat to moderately low and simmer, stirring, until the mixture begins to thicken and its volume has been reduced by a quarter for thinner syrup or a third for thicker syrup, 7 to 10 minutes. Remove from the heat, let cool, cover tightly, and store in the refrigerator for up to 2 weeks.

ICED CARAMEL LATTE

MAKES 1 SERVING • This recipe gives the basic formula for all iced lattes. For a plain one, either eliminate the caramel syrup or, to retain the sweetness, substitute a simple syrup to taste. For iced mocha latte, substitute 1 to 2 tablespoons chocolate syrup. Note: Because hot milk foam may breed bacteria when poured over ice, frothed milk is ordinarily not used in iced lattes and iced cappuccinos.

> **2 rounded tablespoons (about 15 grams) finely ground coffee, preferably an espresso blend**
>
> **Ice cubes**
>
> **2 tablespoons caramel syrup, plus 1 teaspoon for garnish**
>
> **1 cup cold milk (whole or 2%), plus 3 tablespoons milk (whole or evaporated)**

Warm up the espresso machine. Put the coffee in the double-sized filter basket of the portafilter, tamp down with a tamper, and secure the portafilter in the brew head. Place a brew pitcher or other receptacle directly under the brew head, turn on the brew switch, and brew for 22 to 28 seconds to yield 2 to 3 ounces of espresso.

Fill a shaker or lidded jar halfway with ice. Add the 2 tablespoons caramel syrup and 1 cup milk, and top with the freshly brewed espresso.

Quickly cover the shaker (or tightly close the jar lid) and shake well. Pour the contents into a large glass.

Pour the 3 tablespoons whole or evaporated milk in a blender and blend until thickened. Place a spoon over the glass and slowly pour the beaten milk over the spoon. Drizzle with the remaining caramel syrup. Serve immediately.

SPIRITS
AND
COCKTAILS

CARAJILLO

MAKES 1 SERVING • Is it an after-dinner digestive? A nightcap? An eye-opener? An elixir of youth? The alchemy of the *carajillo* (pronounced cah-rah-HEE-oh), an espresso spiked with flambéed brandy, remains a Spanish mystery. A *carajillo* could be a prelude to a siesta or long slumber, yet the sleepless revelers of Madrid enjoy the opposite effect: The jolt they get from a *carajillo* is their second wind. And old-timers drink *carajillos* first thing in the morning, seeking their first wind.

You have two chances to control how much alcohol ends up in any serving: The first is how much brandy you start out with; the second, how much alcohol you allow to burn off. At Spanish cafés they pour the brandy into a small glass over sugar, lemon peel, and a few coffee beans and heat the mixture using the steam nozzle of an espresso machine. After the brandy is ignited and the flame is extinguished with a spoon, espresso is pulled directly into the glass, over the brandy.

1 to 2 teaspoons sugar, optional

3 tablespoons (1½ ounces or 1 jigger) brandy

1-inch piece lemon peel

3 to 4 coffee beans

2 rounded tablespoons (about 15 grams) ground coffee (medium-fine grind for a moka pot, fine grind for an espresso machine)

⅔ cup cold water

Combine the sugar, if desired, with the brandy, lemon peel, and coffee beans in a small saucepan and heat over medium-high heat, stirring, until the sugar is dissolved. Turn off the heat and carefully light the brandy with a long match. Extinguish the receding flame by stirring with a metal spoon.

If using a moka pot, remove the filter basket from the lower chamber and fill the lower chamber with cold water up to the safety valve. Replace the filter and fill with 1 rounded tablespoon coffee for a single-serving pot or 2 rounded tablespoons for a double-serving pot. Gently level the grinds, firmly screw the top section onto the base, and place the pot over the burner. Leave the top lid open and turn the heat to medium-low. When the upper chamber is filled about halfway and the flow from the nozzle begins to sputter, turn off the heat, close the lid, and wait until the chamber is full and the sputtering has stopped. (For a single-serving pot, repeat with the remaining coffee grinds.) If using an espresso machine, put all the coffee in the double-sized filter basket of the portafilter, tamp down with a tamper, and secure the portafilter in the brew head. Place a brew pitcher or other receptacle directly under the brew head, turn on the brew switch, and brew for 22 to 28 seconds to yield 2 to 3 ounces of espresso.

Strain the brandy mixture into a coffee cup, small mug, or small heat-proof glass. Top with the espresso. Serve immediately.

COFFEE LIQUEUR

MAKES 2 QUARTS • Here's a chance to make a liqueur flavored with your favorite coffee. You can substitute brandy for some or all of the vodka for a richer flavor.

> ¾ cup (about 70 grams) ground coffee (fine grind for espresso, medium-coarse grind for French press), preferably a medium-dark or dark roast
>
> 2 cups sugar
>
> ½ vanilla bean, split lengthwise
>
> 3 cups plus 3 tablespoons (one fifth bottle) vodka

Warm up the espresso machine. Put 2 rounded tablespoons of the coffee in the double-sized filter basket of the portafilter, tamp down with a tamper, and secure the portafilter in the brew head. Place a brew pitcher or other receptacle directly under the brew head, turn on the brew switch, and brew for 22 to 28 seconds to yield 3 ounces of espresso. Repeat with the remaining coffee grinds until you have 2 cups of espresso. If using a French press, add the coffee to the pot, pour 2½ cups near-boiling water over the grinds, stir with a wooden spoon, and replace the lid. Let the coffee steep for 4 minutes, then carefully push the plunger down to the bottom of the cylinder. Add the sugar to the espresso or coffee and stir until completely dissolved. Let cool to room temperature.

Place the vanilla bean in a large sterilized jar or container. Pour in the vodka and the sweetened coffee, stir well, and cover tightly. Let the mixture rest in a dark place for 4 weeks.

Pour the liqueur twice through a cheesecloth-lined sieve or a coffee filter to strain out vanilla bean grains and any sediment. Pour into a clean bottle and cap tightly. The liqueur will keep for several months. To serve, pour straight up, over ice, or into coffee.

CAFÉ ALESSANDRO

MAKES 1 SERVING • In the beginning there was the "Alexander," a cocktail of equal parts gin, crème de cacao (chocolate liqueur), and cream. Next there was the "Brandy Alexander," with brandy replacing gin, and later the "Coffee Alexander," which kept the brandy but substituted coffee liqueur for chocolate liqueur. Most interpreters of the "Espresso Alexander" or, more commonly, "Alexander Espresso," have replaced the coffee liqueur with fresh espresso and restored the crème de cacao. Bartender/barista Silvio del Favero of the renowned Schumann's TagesBar ("day bar") in Munich brought that cocktail into the daylight with his milkier, milder, frothy, nutmeg-dusted, latte-colored Café Alessandro.

1 rounded tablespoon (about 7 grams) finely ground coffee,
preferably an espresso blend

2 teaspoons (⅓ ounce) brandy

1 tablespoon (½ ounce) white crème de cacao

4 teaspoons light cream

2 tablespoons whole milk

Ice cubes

A pinch nutmeg

Warm up the espresso machine. Put the coffee in the filter basket of the portafilter, tamp down with a tamper, and secure the portafilter in the brew head. Place a brew pitcher or other receptacle directly under the brew head, turn on the brew switch, and brew for 22 to 28 seconds to yield 1 to 1½ ounces of espresso. Let cool slightly.

Combine the espresso with the brandy, white crème de cacao, cream, and milk in a cocktail shaker, fill with ice, and shake vigorously. Strain into a chilled cocktail glass. Sprinkle with nutmeg. Serve immediately.

IRISH COFFEE

MAKES 2 SERVINGS • According to legend, Irish coffee dates back to 1942, when Joe Sheridan, the restaurant chef at Foynes Airport in Shannon, Ireland, thought to top off hot coffee with a shot of Irish whiskey, all the better to warm a group of transatlantic passengers grounded by bad weather. "Is this Brazilian coffee?" asked a surprised American. "No," replied Sheridan, "it's Irish coffee."

America's first Irish coffee was perfected a decade later at San Francisco's Buena Vista Cafe, which met the challenge of getting the whipped cream to float by aging it for 48 hours (not recommended) and then frothing it to a precise consistency. Cocktail authority Dale DeGroff uses a very cold fresh heavy cream—never canned—and whips or whisks it until not quite stiff, so there are no bubbles and the cream can be slowly poured. (In the original recipe, the heavy cream was not whipped at all.) He sweetens his Irish coffee with a brown-sugar syrup.

5 tablespoons (about 30 grams) ground coffee (medium-fine grind for cone filter, medium grind for flat-bottomed filter, medium-coarse grind for French press)

1¼ cups cold water

2 sugar cubes or 1½ tablespoons Simple Syrup (page 85), preferably made with brown sugar

6 tablespoons (3 ounces or 2 jiggers) Irish whiskey

⅓ to ½ cup unsweetened Whipped Cream (page 32), lightly whipped (or heavy cream)

Place the coffee in the filter of a drip coffeemaker or the pot of a French press. Heat the water to a near boil (195 to 205°F/90 to 95°C). For a manual drip coffeemaker, pour just enough of the water evenly over the

coffee to wet the grinds. Wait 30 seconds, then pour the remaining water over the coffee. If using a French press, place the coffee in the pot, pour the water over the grinds, stir, and cover. Let steep for 4 minutes, then carefully push the plunger down to the bottom of the cylinder, making sure to keep it level.

Rinse two glass mugs or goblets with hot water, then dry them. Place a sugar cube or half the syrup in each, then top first with half the whiskey and then with half the coffee. Stir each with a spoon, finishing the motion by moving the spoon back and forth like a pendulum across the diameter of the glass to stop the spinning of the liquid

Hold a spoon directly over the liquid surface of a glass, pour whipped cream into the spoon, and let it flow gently into the glass. Repeat with the second glass. Serve immediately.

SPANISH COFFEE

MAKES 2 SERVINGS • What the Buena Vista Cafe in San Francisco is to Irish coffee and Antoine's in New Orleans is to *café brûlot*, Huber's in Portland, Oregon, is to Spanish coffee. Established in 1879, named Huber's in 1895, and moved to its present location in 1911, it is by any measure the oldest surviving saloon and restaurant in Portland. In a damp city that still likes its Spanish coffee, that hot-drink holdover from a time when winters were colder, Huber's waiters are the standard-bearers. These indefatigable showmen prepare Spanish coffees tableside, one after another, with great fanfare and pyrotechnics, as if everyone in the room were celebrating birthdays. When the flames have died down and the waiters have moved their act to yet another table, there is plenty of heat left in the glass: The great winter warmer is a coffee spiked with coffee liqueur, triple sec, and 150-proof rum.

5 to 6 tablespoons (about 30 to 35 grams) ground coffee (medium-fine grind for cone filter, medium grind for flat-bottomed filter, medium-coarse grind for French press)

1¼ cups cold water

2 tablespoons lime juice

2 to 4 tablespoons sugar

¼ cup (2 ounces) high-proof rum

2 dashes triple sec

6 tablespoons (3 ounces or 2 jiggers) Kahlúa or other coffee liqueur (page 98)

⅓ to ½ cup Whipped Cream (page 32)

2 small pinches nutmeg

Place the coffee in the filter of a drip coffeemaker or the pot of a French press. Heat the water to a near boil (195 to 205°F/90 to 95°C). If using a manual drip coffeemaker, pour just enough of the water evenly over the coffee to wet the grinds. Wait 30 seconds, then pour the remaining water over the coffee. If using a French press, pour the water over the grinds, stir, and cover. Let steep for 4 minutes, then carefully push the plunger down to the bottom of the cylinder, making sure to keep it level.

Dip two 8- to 10-ounce glass goblets in lime juice and then in sugar to rim the goblets. Working with one goblet at a time, pour in 2 tablespoons rum and 1 dash triple sec. Using a long match, carefully light the liquor, swirling the glass to melt the sugar coating the rim. Pour in 3 tablespoons of Kahlúa, then add half of the brewed coffee.

Hold a spoon directly over the liquid surface of a glass, pour whipped cream into the spoon, and let it flow gently into the glass. Sprinkle with nutmeg. Repeat with the second globlet. Serve immediately.

ALGERIAN COFFEE OF PRAGUE

MAKES 1 SERVING • The Prague part is inserted to indicate that this Viennese-style dessert coffee is a specialty of Prague with no known ties to Algeria. Although flavored with an eggnog liqueur whose production and appeal are largely local, the confection is listed at the Municipal House and other grand and not-so-grand coffeehouses of the Czech Republic capital as *Alžírská káva*—"Algerian coffee." The eggnog liqueur is cloying when sampled on its own, but espresso counters that effect.

> 2 rounded tablespoons (about 15 grams) ground coffee
> (fine grind for espresso, medium-fine grind for moka pot),
> preferably an espresso blend
>
> 3 tablespoons eggnog (substitute zabaglione—see page 64)
>
> 2 teaspoons (⅓ ounce) brandy
>
> Sugar to taste, optional
>
> 1 very large dollop lightly sweetened Whipped Cream (page 32)

If using an espresso machine, put the coffee in the double-sized filter basket of the portafilter, tamp down with a tamper, and secure the portafilter in the brew head. Place a brew pitcher or other receptacle directly under the brew head, turn on the brew switch, and brew for 22 to 28 seconds to yield 3 ounces of espresso. If using a moka pot, remove the filter basket from the lower chamber of a moka pot and fill the lower chamber with cold water up to the safety valve. Replace the filter and fill with 1 rounded tablespoon for a single-serving pot, 2 rounded tablespoons for a double-serving pot. Gently level the grinds, firmly screw the top section onto the base, and place the pot over the burner. Leave the top lid open and turn the heat to medium-low. When the upper chamber is filled about halfway and the flow from the nozzle begins to sputter, turn off the heat and wait until the chamber is full and the sputtering has stopped. (If using a single-serving pot, repeat with the remaining coffee grinds.)

Rinse a tall, stemmed dessert glass or glass mug with hot water, then dry it.

Combine the eggnog and brandy in a bowl and beat with a whisk. Pour or spoon the mixture into the glass. Stir sugar into the espresso, if desired, and pour over the eggnog mixture. Top very generously with whipped cream, and serve.

CAFÉ BRÛLOT

MAKES 4 SERVINGS • The French word *brûlot*, from the verb *brûler* (to burn), can refer either to a small fireship with enough fuel to incinerate an enemy position or a sweetened, flambéed brandy. In New Orleans, the *café brûlot* is pretty much both those things. The sweet, spiced after-dinner coffee is a specialty of classic French Quarter restaurants like Antoine's.

The traditional presentation entails a tableside fireworks of great daring and agility: The flaming coffee-brandy mixture is ladled over a spiral of orange peel, creating a dazzling ribbon of fire. The following recipe dims the fireworks some, but not the spice.

> ½ cup (about 45 grams) ground coffee (medium-fine grind for cone filter, medium grind for flat-bottomed filter, medium-coarse grind for French press)
>
> 2½ cups water
>
> 1 orange peel, cut into 1-inch strips
>
> ¼ cup (2 ounces) brandy
>
> 2 tablespoons sugar
>
> 6 whole cloves
>
> 2 cinnamon sticks

Place the coffee in the filter of a drip coffeemaker or the pot of a French press. Heat the water to a near boil (195 to 205°F/90 to 95°C). For a manual drip coffeemaker, pour just enough of the water evenly over the coffee to wet the grinds. Wait 30 seconds, then pour the remaining water over the coffee. If using a French press, pour the water over the grinds, stir, and cover. Let steep for 4 minutes, then carefully push the plunger down to the bottom of the cylinder, making sure to keep it level.

Combine the orange peel strips, brandy, sugar, cloves, and cinnamon in a saucepan over medium heat and cook—but do not boil—until the sugar is dissolved.

Using a long match, carefully set the brandy mixture aflame. Gradually add the coffee to douse the flames, strain into four small cups, and serve immediately.

Passing the Café Brûlot Torch

The New Orleans restaurant Antoine's cannot truly claim its café brûlot recipe to be definitive since even its celebrated waiters don't agree on the proportions. "Every waiter makes it differently," says James Campora, an Antoine's waiter since 1982.

The original formula was created in the 1890s by Antoine's chef Jules Alciatore, the son of the restaurant's eponymous founder, Antoine Alciatore. While apprenticing in France, Jules was likely enthralled by the blue flames of the *Brûlot Charentais*, a flambéed coffee from the Cognac region. Appealing to the appetite for spice and spectacle back home in New Orleans, the younger Alciatore seasoned his variation with cinnamon and cloves and ignited it in a silver bowl. The flaming brûlot torch was passed from waiter to waiter.

The late Sammy LeBlanc, an Antoine's waiter for fifty-four years, taught Campora how to make the flames dance over the tablecloth. Only once has the protégé set fire to a diner's jacket. "He didn't get hurt or anything," recalls Campora, "but he sure seemed nervous."

COFFEE NOG

MAKES 1 SERVING · Long before there were eggnog lattes to quaff during the holiday season, we had cold coffee nogs to wake up with on Christmas mornings—some with alcohol, some without. In the 1890s, James Walker Tufts, a Boston manufacturer of soda fountain equipment, published a recipe for coffee nog in the updated edition of his *Book of Directions*. Although his formula called for an uncooked egg, in this adaptation the egg is heated with milk to kill off bacteria and avoid any risk of food-borne illness. Tufts also included a recipe for egg coffee, which is similar to a coffee nog except that spring water and cream are used instead of Port and milk. Perhaps the thinking of the time was that if you can't have the Port, at least you are entitled to the guilty pleasure of the cream.

1 rounded tablespoon (about 7 grams) ground coffee
(fine grind for espresso, medium-fine grind for moka pot),
preferably an espresso blend

1 egg, beaten

½ cup milk

1½ tablespoons Simple Syrup (page 85)

2 tablespoons (1 ounce) Port (or substitute rum)

¾ cup crushed ice

If using an espresso machine, put the coffee in the filter basket of the portafilter, tamp down with a tamper, and secure the portafilter in the brew head. Place a brew pitcher or other receptacle directly under the brew head, turn on the brew switch, and brew for 22 to 28 seconds to yield 1½ ounces of espresso. If using a single-serving moka pot, remove the filter basket from the lower chamber and fill the lower chamber with cold water (about ⅓ cup) up to the safety valve. Replace the filter and fill with the coffee. Gently level the grinds, firmly screw the top section onto the base, and place the pot over the burner. Leave the top lid open and turn the heat to medium-low. When the upper chamber is filled about halfway and the flow from the nozzle begins to sputter, close the lid and turn off the heat.

Combine the egg and milk in a bowl and mix well. Transfer to a small saucepan and heat over low heat to a temperature of 160°F (about 70°C). Do not overheat, or the egg will curdle. Remove from the heat and let cool for a few minutes.

Combine the egg-milk mixture, syrup, espresso, Port, and crushed ice in a shaker and shake well. Pour all the contents into a tall glass tumbler (about 14 ounces). Serve immediately.

EGGNOG LATTE

MAKE 1 SERVING • To satisfy anyone who regards the use of store-bought eggnog as an act of betrayal against family tradition or good taste, this recipe begins with directions for preparing homemade eggnog. Since the mixture calls for a raw egg, be sure to heat it to 160°F (about 70°C) to kill any bacteria and cut the risk of food-borne illness.

Those of you who embrace the convenience of ready-made eggnog can prepare their lattes with nonalcoholic eggnog from such brands as Borden and Southern Comfort. Simply mix the eggnog with the same quantity of milk (or, for a more strongly flavored latte, half the quantity of milk) and stir in bourbon, if desired, before steaming the mixture.

You can bring eggnog flavor and warmth to your latte in a single stroke by eliminating the eggnog and bourbon altogether and enriching the milk instead with a shot or two of eggnog liqueur from such brands as Old New England, Pennsylvania Dutch, and McCormick Irish.

¾ cup milk (whole or 2%)

1 egg yolk

2 teaspoons sugar

1 tablespoon rum

1 tablespoon bourbon

1 small pinch ground nutmeg, plus more for garnish

2 rounded tablespoons (about 15 grams) ground coffee
(fine grind for espresso, medium-fine grind for moka pot),
preferably an espresso blend

Heat, but do not boil, ¼ cup of the milk in a saucepan or with the steam wand of an espresso machine.

Combine the egg yolk and sugar in a bowl and beat with a whisk. Gradually pour in the heated milk, whisking until the mixture is homogeneous. Add the remaining milk, rum, bourbon, and the pinch of nutmeg and mix well.

If using an espresso machine, put the coffee in the double-sized filter basket of the portafilter, tamp down with a tamper, and secure the portafilter in the brew head. Place a brew pitcher or other receptacle directly under the brew head, turn on the brew switch, and brew for 22 to 28 seconds to yield 3 ounces of espresso. If using a moka pot, remove the filter basket from the lower chamber and fill the lower chamber with cold water up to the safety valve. Replace the filter and fill with 1 rounded tablespoon for a single-serving pot, 2 rounded tablespoons for a double-serving pot. Gently level the grinds, firmly screw the top section onto the base, and place the pot over the burner. Leave the top lid open and turn the heat to medium-low. When the upper chamber is filled about halfway and the flow from the nozzle begins to sputter, turn off the heat and wait until the chamber is full and the sputtering has stopped. (If using a single-serving pot, repeat with the remaining coffee grinds.)

Steam the eggnog mixture with the steam wand of an espresso machine, or heat it in a saucepan to a temperature of 160°F (about 70°C). Do not make it any hotter, or the egg may curdle. If using a saucepan, froth the heated milk with a handheld frother.

Pour the espresso into a mug or glass. Top with the steamed eggnog and sprinkle the foam with nutmeg. Serve immediately.

SLAVIA MACCHIATO

• In the back of the Prague's historic Café Slavia, just to the right of the corner window table that was Václav Havel's favorite, hangs Viktor Oliva's *Absinthe Drinker*. The Czech painter (1861–1928) portrayed a quintessential Bohemian in his element: A zonked man with a glass of absinthe is visited by a green apparition who sits, naked and nymphlike, on his table. Absinthe, an anise-flavored liquor known in Oliva's time as the Green Fairy, is closely associated with Bohemian decadence. Distilled from wormwood and thought to make men go mad, absinthe was outlawed in various countries during the 1910s and 1920s. Its recent revival roughly coincided with the reopening in 1998 of Café Slavia, which had been shuttered for seven years. Absinthe is poured into the café's new eponymous coffee, the Slavia *macchiato*. The pale green drink is a good match for the huge clock that glows in green over the "bus stop" (service counter), as well as the mystery nymph seated on her favorite table.

> 1½ ounces (1 jigger) absinthe
>
> ⅔ cup whole milk
>
> 2 rounded tablespoons (about 15 grams) ground coffee, preferably an espresso blend
>
> Simple Syrup (page 85) to taste, optional

Warm up the espresso machine. Pour the absinthe into a heatproof 10-ounce glass. Press the steam switch and wait for the ready indicator to light up. Meanwhile, pour the milk into a stainless steel pitcher. Submerge the tip of the steam wand at least half an inch below the milk surface and turn on the steam switch. As the foam rises, gradually lower the pitcher so the tip of the wand remains just below the milk surface. As the milk

begins to heat up, tilt the pitcher slightly to swirl the milk and continue to steam until the side of the pitcher becomes too hot to hold. Turn off the steam while still holding the tip of the wand under the milk surface.

Spoon the frothed milk into the glass over the absinthe, starting with the foam on top and gradually working your way down until the glass is full. Let stand, allowing the milk to settle under the foam while you prepare the espresso.

Put the coffee in the double-sized filter basket of the portafilter, tamp down with a tamper, and secure the portafilter in the brew head. Place a brewing pitcher or other receptacle directly under the brew head, turn on the brew switch, and brew for 22 to 28 seconds to yield 3 ounces of espresso.

Very, very slowly pour the espresso into the glass directly over the foam in a thin stream. Top, if desired, with simple syrup. Serve immediately.

Vodka Espresso

When You Need a Coffee AND a Drink

I T WAS LUNCHTIME IN LONDON'S West End, and Dick Bradsell was mixing the day's first cocktails at the Soho Brasserie when a famous fashion model approached the bar with an urgency perhaps ill suited to the Queen's English. She requested a drink that would "wake me up and f*** me up." The bartender obliged. Making use of the restaurant's espresso machine, a rarity at London bars in the mid-1980s, Bradsell poured a shaken mixture of vodka, espresso, and sugar over ice in a highball glass, producing a dark-brown beverage with a creamy tan head similar in appearance to a Guinness. Achieving at least one and likely both of the desired effects, a modern classic was born. "It's hardcore, it's black and white, it's nasty," notes Bradsell, a bartender from the old school, enumerating his cocktail's virtues or, if you prefer, vices.

The vodka espresso did not become truly iconic until Bradsell worked with a colleague, who goes by the singular name Vasco, at Match Bar in London's Clerkenwell district, to refine the recipe and add what has become its signature garnish: three coffee beans. The elegant Vasco variation derives its coffee power from three sources: espresso, Tia Maria coffee liqueur, and Kahlúa coffee liqueur. Bradsell may no longer be associated with Match Bar, but he is clearly honored to have his name stenciled prominently on the bar's wall and prouder still to know the words "vodka espresso" are printed beside it. The bar, like Bradsell himself but few others, has resisted the fashion dictating that the word *martini* be attached to any cocktail served in a V-shaped glass. The plethora of espresso martinis notwithstanding, Bradsell applauds the cocktail craze that crossed the pond from New York to London in the 1990s and helped make him something of a cocktail guru, even if he's never been deceived by a public that confers rock-star status upon bartenders. "You're just doing bloody drinks," he says. "We are servants. If you don't remember that, they'll make you remember."

VODKA ESPRESSO

MAKES 1 SERVING • A vodka espresso would be called an espresso martini by many, but the bartender-creator Dick Bradsell wanted to avoid the cliché. See the variation for his simple version. This more elaborate version of the original requires two types of coffee liqueur, with the drier Tia Maria acting as a foil for the sweeter, richer Kahlúa. Yet what the cocktail needs much more than any particular brand or brands of liqueur is the flavor and body of a high-quality espresso prepared to [continued on page 116]

full strength. Diluting the espresso with water will only make it taste bitter. "If the espresso is too strong," quips Bradsell, "add more vodka."

> 1 rounded tablespoon (about 7 grams) finely ground coffee, preferably an espresso blend
>
> 3 tablespoons (1½ ounces or 1 jigger) vodka
>
> 1½ tablespoons (¾ ounce) Kahlúa (or substitute any coffee liqueur)
>
> 1½ tablespoons (¾ ounce) Tia Maria (or substitute any coffee liqueur)
>
> Ice cubes
>
> 3 roasted coffee beans

Warm up the espresso machine. Put the coffee in the filter basket of the portafilter, tamp down with a tamper, and secure the portafilter in the brew head. Place a brewing pitcher or other receptacle directly under the brew head, turn on the brew switch, and brew for 22 to 28 seconds to yield 1½ ounces of espresso. Let cool to room temperature, then refrigerate until ready to use.

Combine the espresso with the vodka, Kahlúa, and Tia Maria in a cocktail shaker, fill with ice, and shake vigorously. Strain into a chilled cocktail glass, and garnish with the coffee beans. Serve immediately.

Original Vodka Espresso: Prepare the espresso with 2 rounded tablespoons (about 15 grams) finely ground coffee. Instead of the liqueurs, add 2 teaspoons of Simple Syrup (page 85) to the espresso in the cocktail shaker. Pour over ice in a highball glass and serve.

ESPRESSO PLATINO

• For cocktail consultant Ryan Magarian, the problem with espresso martinis isn't the espresso; it's the vodka. The mixologist would rather base his cocktail creations on a spirit with real flavor—rum, gin, or tequila, for instance. "Vodka is like chicken or tofu," he complains. Gin doesn't work too well with coffee flavor, hence all the espresso martinis made with vodka, but Magarian thinks the balance of acidity and fruitiness in fine tequila marries well with the espresso. He developed the Espresso Platino for the Hyde Lounge in Los Angeles as part of an El Tesoro Platinum tequila promotion.

> 1 rounded tablespoon (about 7 grams) finely ground coffee, preferably an espresso blend
>
> 2 tablespoons (1 ounce) El Tesoro Platinum tequila or other fine tequila
>
> 2 tablespoons (1 ounce) Starbucks Coffee Liqueur (or substitute any coffee liqueur)
>
> 2 tablespoons (1 ounce) Simple Syrup (page 85)
>
> Ice cubes
>
> 3 roasted coffee beans, for garnish

Warm up the espresso machine. Put the coffee in the filter basket of the portafilter, tamp down with a tamper, and secure the portafilter in the brew head. Place a brewing pitcher or other receptacle directly under the brew head, turn on the brew switch, and brew for 22 to 28 seconds to yield 1 to 1½ ounces of espresso. Let cool to room temperature.

Combine the espresso with the tequila, coffee liqueur, and simple syrup in a cocktail shaker. Fill with ice and shake vigorously for 6 seconds. Strain into a chilled cocktail glass, garnish with the roasted coffee beans, and serve.

INDEX